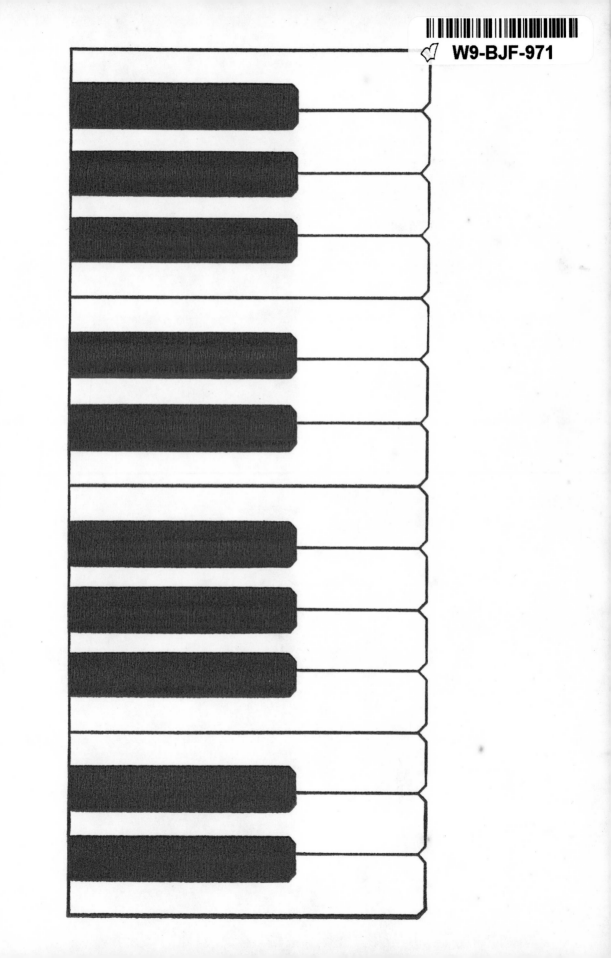

SILVER BURDETT music

ELIZABETH CROOK
BENNETT REIMER
DAVID S. WALKER

SILVER BURDETT COMPANY

MORRISTOWN, NEW JERSEY · GLENVIEW, ILLINOIS
PALO ALTO · DALLAS · ATLANTA

SPECIAL CONTRIBUTORS

William M. Anderson (non-Western music), Aurora, Ohio

Kojo Fosu Baiden (music of Africa), Silver Springs, Maryland

Dulce B. Bohn (recorder), Wilmington, Delaware

Charles L. Boilès (music of Mexico), Bloomington, Indiana

Ian L. Bradley (Canadian music), Victoria, British Columbia, Canada

Gerald Burakoff (recorder), Levittown, New York

Henry Burnett (music of Japan), Flushing, Long Island, New York

Richard J. Colwell (testing and evaluation), Urbana, Illinois

Marilyn C. Davidson (music for Orff instruments), Bergenfield, New Jersey

Joan Davies (music of Canada and Japan), Charlottetown, P.E.I., Canada

Kay Hardesty (special education), Chautauqua, New York

James M. Harris (music in early childhood), San Francisco, California

Doris E. Hays (avant-garde music), New York City

Nazir A. Jairazbhoy (music of India), Windsor, Ontario, Canada

Maria Jordan (music of Greece), Hicksville, Long Island, New York

Robert A. Kauffman (music of Africa), Seattle, Washington

Edna Knock (music of Canada), Brandon, Manitoba, Canada

John Lidstone (visual arts), Brooklyn, New York

David McHugh (youth music), New York City

Alan P. Merriam (music of the North American Indians), Bloomington, Indiana

Lucille Mitchell (American folk songs), Alexandria, Virginia

Maria Luisa Muñoz (music of Puerto Rico), Houston, Texas

Lynn Freeman Olson (listening program), New York City

Mary E. Perrin (music in the inner city), Chicago, Illinois

Carmino Ravosa (children's song literature), Briarcliff Manor, New York

Joyce Bogusky-Reimer (avant-garde music), Wilmette, Illinois

Geraldine Slaughter (music of Africa), Washington, D.C.

Mark Slobin (music of the Near East), Middletown, Connecticut

Ruth Marie Stone (music of Africa), New York City

Leona B. Wilkins (music in the inner city), Evanston, Illinois

CONSULTANTS

Lynn Arizzi (levels 1 and 2), Reston, Virginia

Joy Browne (levels 5 and 6), Kansas City, Missouri

Nancy Crump, classroom teacher, Alexandria, Louisiana

Lyla Evans, classroom teacher, South Euclid, Ohio

Catherine Gallas, classroom teacher, Bridgeton, Missouri

Linda Haselton, classroom teacher, Westminster, California

Ruth A. Held, classroom teacher, Lancaster, Pennsylvania

Judy F. Jackson, classroom teacher, Franklin, Tennessee

Mary E. Justice, Auburn University, Auburn, Alabama

Jean Lembke (levels 3 and 4), Tonawanda, New York

Barbara Nelson, classroom teacher, Baytown, Texas

Terry Philips (youth music), New York City

Ruth Red, Director of Music Education, Houston, Texas

Mary Ann Shealy (levels 1 and 2), Florence, South Carolina

Beatrice Schattschneider (levels 1–6), Morristown, New Jersey

Paulette Schmalz, classroom teacher, Phoenix, Arizona

Sister Helen C. Schneider, Clarke College, Dubuque, Iowa

Merrill Staton (recordings), Alpine, New Jersey

ACKNOWLEDGMENTS

The authors and editors of SILVER BURDETT MUSIC acknowledge with gratitude the contributions of the following persons.

Marjorie Hahn, New York
Yoriko Kozumi, Japan
Ruth Merrill, Texas
Mary Ann Nelson, Texas
Bennie Mae Oliver, Texas
Joanne Ryan, New York
Helen Spiers, Virginia
Shirley Ventrone, Rhode Island
Avonelle Walker, New York

Credit and appreciation are due publishers and copyright owners for use of the following.

"African Dance" copyright 1926 by Alfred A. Knopf, Inc., renewed 1954 by Langston Hughes. From SELECTED POEMS of Langston Hughes. Reprinted by permission of Alfred A. Knopf, Inc.

"Night" from COLLECTED POEMS by Sara Teasdale. Copyright 1930 by Sara Teasdale Filsinger, renewed 1958 by Guaranty Trust Co. of New York, Executor. Reprinted by permission of Macmillan Publishing Co., Inc.

"The Night Will Never Stay" from ELEANOR FARJEON'S POEMS FOR CHILDREN. Copyright 1951 by Eleanor Farjeon. Renewed 1979 by Gervase Farjeon. By permission of J.B. Lippincott, Publisher and Harold Ober Associates.

"Snatch of Sliphorn Jazz" from GOOD MORNING AMERICA, copyright, 1928, 1956, by Carl Sandburg. Reprinted by permission of Harcourt Brace Jovanovich, Inc.

CONTENTS

SECTION 1: TONE COLOR

INTRODUCTION TO TONE COLOR

Music is made of sounds and silences. There are many different kinds of sounds (tone colors) and many different ways to combine them. Because of this, we will probably never run out of interesting ways to create music with a variety of tone colors.

Some of the tone colors suggested by the photographs on these pages are familiar. Others may be less familiar. In this section you will review some things you know about how tone colors are used in music. You will also learn a few new things about tone color.

Natural Sounds

Bring in one or two of your records from home to share with others. Can you hear the tone colors that are used in the music?

As you listen to this recording, keep time to the steady beat by using the tone color of natural sounds—clapping, snapping, tapping.

◉ *Porcupine Rock*
1

Add the tone color of natural sounds as you listen to the recording of this song.

JOY TO THE WORLD WORDS AND MUSIC BY HOYT AXTON ◉ 1

COPYRIGHT © 1970 BY LADY JANE MUSIC. USED BY PERMISSION.

1. Jer - e - mi - ah was   a bull - frog,   was a good__ friend of

mine.   Nev - er un - der - stood a sin - gle word he   said,___ but we

2. If I were the king of the world, tell you what I'd do,

Throw away the fears and the tears and the jeers,

And have a good time with you.

Yes, I'll have a good time with you. *Refrain*

For percussion parts, see p. 223.

Natural Sounds

Listen for tone color in this recording. Who sings the solo and
who sings the chorus parts? When you can, add the tone color
of your voice on the chorus parts.

CUM-MA-LA BE-STAY

WORDS AND MUSIC BY DONNY BURKE, JERRY VANCE, AND TERRY PHILIPS

© 1972 BY POPDRAW MUSIC CORP., NEW YORK, NEW YORK

SOLO   CHORUS

Bam - a - lam - a - cum-ma-la, Cum-ma-la be - stay. Bam - a - lam - a-cum-ma-la,

SOLO

Cum-ma - la be - stay. Bam - a-lam - a-cum-ma-la, Cum-ma-la be - stay.

CHORUS   SOLO   In the

Bam - a - lam - a - cum - ma - la, Cum - ma - la be - stay.

sum-mer - time__ when the sun goes down And the heat starts ris - ing

off the ground,__ My friends and I we gath-er round,__ We

CHORUS

dance and sing to the cum-ma - la sound. Cum-ma-la sound,

SOLO   ALL

Cum-ma - la sound. Ev - 'ry - bod - y forms a cir - cle;__

Now some - bod - y jumps in-side.__ (Solo singer jumps inside circle.) You

clap your hands, You stamp your feet,____

You do the jerk To the cum-ma-la beat.____

SOLO

CHORUS

Bam-a-lam-a-cum-ma-la, Cum-ma-la be-stay. Bam-a-lam-a-cum-ma-la,

SOLO

Cum-ma-la be-stay. Bam-a-lam-a-cum-ma-la, Cum-ma-la be-stay.

ALL

Bam-a-lam-a-cum-ma-la, Cum-ma-la be-stay.

Use the rhythm pattern of the first solo part and make up a hand jive. Use a natural sound—clap, snap, tap, or make up a sound of your own. These examples will help you get started.

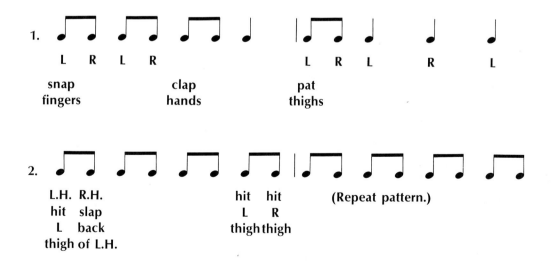

1. L R L R   L R L R L

snap   clap   pat
fingers   hands   thighs

2. L.H. R.H.   hit hit   (Repeat pattern.)
   hit slap   L R
   L back   thigh thigh
   thigh of L.H.

Now, play your hand jive all through the song.

Natural Sounds

There are some natural sounds used in the recording of
"Shoeflies." Can you discover what they are?

SHOEFLIES   WORDS AND MUSIC BY BOB SAKAYAMA

© 1972 EARTHLING MUSIC. REPRINTED BY PERMISSION.

Shoe-flies fast-er than me, ___ I got-ta run, run, run, ___ or

I won't sit. ___ And when the man says, "Dig my foot,"

Shoe-flies. ___ Dom - i - noes ___

more than I do, ___ and there's a chance that he may real-ly ev-en

know more than you, ___ And when the man says,

"I don't know what to do," Dom - i - noes. ___

But - ter - flies ___ ov - er the hill, ___

You can't find____ it then no - bod - y will.____

And when the man says, "Bake my bread,"____ But - ter - flies.____

Here is another version of "Shoeflies," performed by the composer.

Sakayama: *Shoeflies*

LINE DANCE
R means right foot; L means left foot.

Pattern A
   Step backward R, L, R. Touch L next to R (4 beats).
   Step forward L, R, L. Touch R next to L (4 beats).
   Repeat backward and forward pattern (8 beats).

Pattern B
   Step sideways R, L, R. Touch L next to R (4 beats).
   Step sideways L, R, L. Touch R next to L (4 beats).
   Repeat R and L sideways pattern (8 beats).

Pattern C
   Jump forward and hold for one beat (2 beats).
   Jump backward and hold for one beat (2 beats).
   Jump forward, then backward (2 beats).
   Click heels twice and turn to face in another direction.

Repeat the dance.

Using . . . Tone Color 9

Natural Sounds

Some people add the tone color of heel-tapping as an accompaniment to a song. Try tapping heels, one after the other, as you listen to this song. Tap the steady beat—two beats in each measure.

I'SE THE B'Y

FOLK SONG FROM NEWFOUNDLAND   NEW WORDS AND NEW MUSIC ADAPTATION BY OSCAR BRAND

TRO—© Copyright 1957 Hollis Music, Inc., New York, N.Y. Used by permission.

1. I'se the b'y that builds the boat, I'se the b'y that sails her.
2. I took Li - za to the dance; Faith, but she could trav - el.
3. Su - san White is out of sight, Hid - ing like Jack Hor - ner.

I'se the b'y that catch-es the fish And brings them home to Li - za.
Ev - 'ry step that Li - za took —— Covered an acre of grav - el.
Choose a lad and take —— him back, —— Kiss him in the cor - ner.

REFRAIN

Swing your part - ner, Sal - ly Tib - ble, Swing your part - ner, Sal - ly Brown.

Swing your part - ner, ev - 'ry - one, All a - round —— the cir - cle.

Now try heel-tapping a rhythm pattern in 6/8 meter to accompany the song.

For percussion parts, see p. 226.

10 Using . . . Tone Color

Listen for the different ways that natural
sounds (clapping, stamping, patting, and
heel-tapping) are used in this music.
Can you identify each sound?

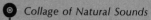 *Collage of Natural Sounds*

Natural Sounds

Fill in all the long sounds by clapping, snapping, or tapping a pattern of your own.

Another time, add movement to your pattern of sound during the long sounds in the song.

GINGELE   WORDS AND MUSIC BY ASTRUD GILBERTO

© 1972 BY POPDRAW MUSIC CORP. & GREGMAR MUSIC, NEW YORK, NEW YORK

Gin - ge - le, ye - le, _____ Gin - ge - le, ye - la. _____

Gin - ge - le, ye - le, _____ Gin - ge - le, ye - la. _____

If you give me Gin - ge - le, I will give you Gin - ge - le.

If you give me Gin - ge - la, I will give you Gin - ge -

la. Gin - ge - le, ye - le, _____ Gin - ge - le, ye - la. _____

Gin - ge - le, ye - le, _____ Gin - ge - le, ye - la. _____

Percussion

Practice one of these percussion parts to play as an accompaniment for "Gingele." Notice how you can change the tone color by playing the same instrument in different ways. For notes with down stems, hold the cowbell with cupped hand. For notes with up stems, hold the cowbell with open hand.

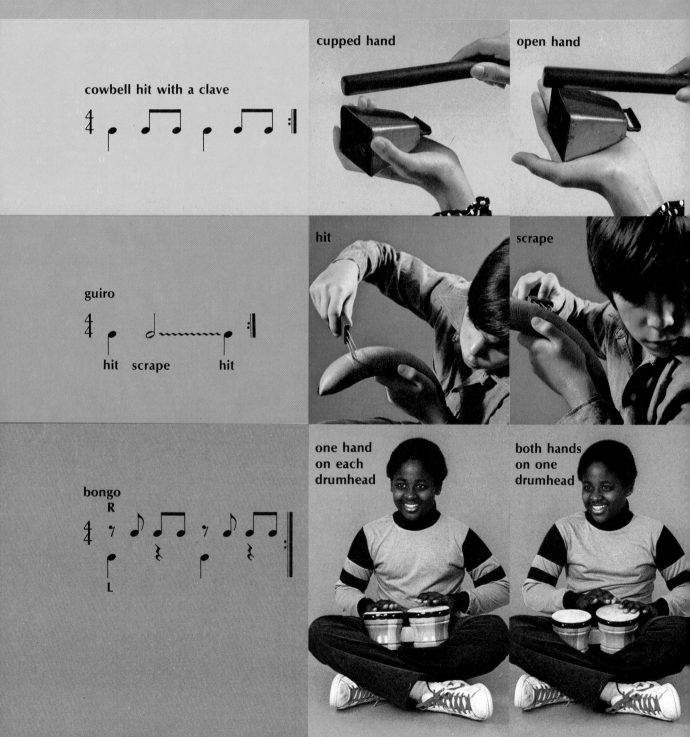

cowbell hit with a clave

cupped hand

open hand

guiro

hit   scrape   hit

hit

scrape

bongo

R

L

one hand on each drumhead

both hands on one drumhead

Percussion

Listen for the tone color of the maracas on the recording of this song.

THE JOHN B. SAILS
FOLK SONG FROM THE BAHAMA ISLANDS

1. Oh, we come on the sloop *John B.* My grand-fa-ther and me, A-round Nas-sau Town we did roam. Walk-in' all night Just see-in' the sights, Well, I feel so break up, I want to go home.

2. The first mate he got sad, Feel-in' aw-f'ly bad, Captain come a-board, took him a-way. Please let me a-lone And let me go home, Well, I feel so break up, I want to go home.

3. The poor cook he got fits, And throw way all the grits, Then he took and eat up all of the corn. Please let me go home, I want to go home, Well, this is the worst trip Since I was born.

REFRAIN

So hoist up___ the *John B.* sails,

See how___ the main - s'l set, Send for___ the Cap-t'n a -

shore, Let___ me go home. Please let___ me go

home, I want___ to go home. Well,___ I

feel so break___ up,___ I want___ to go home.

For a percussion ensemble, see p. 232.

Now play one of these parts to accompany the song.

maracas

claves

You can add the tone color of bongo drum, cowbell, and guiro
by playing one of the parts on page 13 in your book.

Using . . . Tone Color   15

Percussion

The percussion parts on pages 13 and 15 can be used to accompany this song from the West Indies. Practice one of the parts, then plan a combo with others in your class.

LIMBO SONG FROM THE WEST INDIES

FROM SONGS FROM TRINIDAD (EDRIC CONNOR)   COPYRIGHT 1958 BY THE OXFORD UNIVERSITY PRESS

SOLO   *CHORUS*

I want some-bod-y to lim-bo like me, Lim - bo,____ to lim-bo like me.

SOLO   *CHORUS*   *SOLO*

Lim - bo, lim - bo, to lim-bo like me, Lim - bo,____ to lim-bo like me. I

CHORUS

want a girl to lim-bo like this boy, Lim - bo,____ to lim-bo like me.

SOLO   *CHORUS*   *SOLO*

Lim - bo, lim - bo, to lim-bo like this boy, Lim - bo, lim-bo like me. I

CHORUS   *SOLO*

want some-bod-y to lim - bo like me, Lim - bo,____ to lim-bo like me. The

CHORUS

girl must be good to lim - bo like this boy, Lim - bo,____ to lim-bo like me,

SOLO   CHORUS

Lim - bo, lim - bo, to lim-bo like me, Lim - bo,_____ to lim-bo like me,

SOLO   CHORUS

Lim - bo, lim - bo, to lim-bo like this boy, Lim - bo,_____ to lim-bo like me.

Try to do the limbo. Each dancer struts under a pole that is held by two people. After everyone has had a turn, the pole is lowered. Every time the pole is lowered, each dancer must bend further backward to avoid touching the pole. The trick is to strut under the pole without falling.

People in Trinidad do the limbo to music played by a steel band. Listen to this recording of a steel band.

◉ *Highlife*

Using . . . Tone Color   17

CALL CHART 1: Percussion ⊚

You will hear a variety of tone colors made on a snare drum in this recording. Follow each chart as you listen. It will help you hear what is going on in the music.

Benson: "Cretan Dance"

Benson: "Fandango"

1 With snares off, drumhead is hit in center for low sound; near edge for higher sound.

1 Drum is played with snares on.

2 Tone color of sticks struck together in air is added to low and high sounds made on drumhead.

2 Right stick hits left stick, which rests loosely on drumhead, causing it to rebound.

3 Sticks struck together in air, first held tightly and then held loosely to create different tone colors.

3 Sticks struck together in air, first held tightly and then held loosely to create different tone colors.

The Voice

Your voice has a special tone color whether you whisper, speak, shout, or sing.

Listen to how the reader uses the tone color of his voice to help express the meaning of the poem.

For another experience with vocal tone color, see p. 246.

Sandburg: *Snatch of Sliphorn Jazz*

SNATCH OF SLIPHORN JAZZ

Are you happy? It's the only
way to be, kid.
Yes, be happy, it's a good nice
way to be.
But not happy-happy, kid, don't
be too doubled-up doggone happy.
It's the doubled-up doggone happy-
happy people . . . bust hard . . . they
do bust hard . . . when they bust.
Be happy, kid, go to it, but not too
doggone happy.

Carl Sandburg.

How will you use the tone color of your voice to help express the meaning of the poem?

The Voice

Each singing voice, as well as each speaking voice, has its own tone color. Add the tone color of your voice to the voices on the recording in section A of the song.

GONNA SING BLACK SPIRITUAL

Oh, I'm a - gon - na sing, gon - na sing, gon - na

sing all a - long____ the way. Oh, I'm a - gon - na sing, gon - na

sing gon - na sing all a - long the way. way.

1. One day you'll hear the trum - pet sound, gon-na sing all a - long the
2. Oh, Jor - dan's stream is wide and cold,

way. The trum - pet sound the world a - round, gon - na
It chills the body but not the soul,

D.C. al Fine

sing all a - long the way.

Use a percussion instrument and play this rhythm echo during every dotted half note (𝅗𝅥.) in section A of "Gonna Sing."

Now sing or play on the bells a melody echo during the dotted half notes. You will use the following patterns.

gon - na sing   gon - na sing

Listen for the tone color of the voices on the recording of "Its Not that Nina's Naughty." Notice that the voices sing faster and faster. This is called *accelerando*.

IT'S NOT THAT NINA'S NAUGHTY

WORDS AND MUSIC BY LUIGI ZANINELLI

It's not that Ni - na's naugh - ty,   It's not that Ni - na's bad,   It's

just that trou - ble finds her,   No mat - ter where we hides her.

Sing this part until all parts of the round are finished.

No mat - ter where we hides her.

SOUND PIECE 1: Whistle Whatever, Hum However   BETH CROOK

You have a speaking voice, a singing voice, a shouting voice, a whispering voice. How many other sounds can you make with your voice? Here are some suggestions.

(Lip buzz)

(Animal sound)

(Gurgle)

(Hiss)

(Cough)

(Cheek or lip pop)

(Tongue clicks)

(Swoops)

(Whisper)

(Bird call)   (Whistle)   (Hum)

Choose three or more sounds you like best.

Start to create a sound piece by inventing a notation for each sound. Then make a score by arranging the sounds to make a line of different tone colors.

Plan the length of each sound so that the line is about fifteen seconds long. Here is an example.

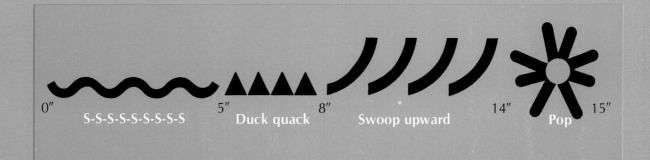

0"   5"   8"   14"   15"
S-S-S-S-S-S-S-S-S   Duck quack   Swoop upward   Pop

When you can feel the length of the line without timing it, perform the piece as a two- or three-part round. When will each part enter?   📖 For another experience with vocal tone color, see p. 242.

After performing your Sound Piece, listen to the recording of "Love for Two Cats" to discover what sounds are used.

🎵 Ravel: "Love for Two Cats"

STYLES: MEDIA IN DIFFERENT
PERIODS OF HISTORY

Music is made of sounds. Throughout history, people have searched for tools (instruments) that make sounds in expressive ways.

Look at the pictures as you listen to the recording. Match the sound with its picture. Each instrument is an important part of the music of its time.

Collage of Sounds
2

24

In every period of history new instruments are invented that reflect the technology of the time. Some instruments continue to be used, while others are popular for shorter periods of time.

What sound-producing instruments do you think technology will inspire next?

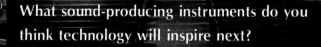

MORE ABOUT TONE COLOR

The Autoharp

Use the tone color of the Autoharp to accompany "La Raspa."
You will use two chords—G and D_7. Play the chords in the $\frac{4}{4}$
pattern shown below the song.

For percussion parts, see p. 222.

LA RASPA   FOLK SONG FROM MEXICO   ENGLISH VERSION BY ROSEMARY JACQUES

Now work of the day is done, And un-der the set-ting sun,
The band plays a live-ly beat, A-mi-gos, a-mi-gas meet,

The mu-sic calls ev-'ry-one To come join in all the fun.
And soon cou-ples fill the street With sounds of their danc-ing feet.

Their voic-es are lift-ed in hap-py song, No-bod-y has a care;

And peo-ple re-joice that the night is long, Laugh-ter is ev-'ry-where.

For a special Autoharp strum, play short strokes with your
thumb on the lowest strings for the notes with stems down. For
notes with stems up, brush the strings in the opposite direction
with your fingers.

THERE'S A FIESTA

FOLK SONG FROM SPAIN   ENGLISH VERSION BY ROSEMARY JACQUES

"MORENA MIA" (JOTA) FROM FOLK MUSIC AND POETRY OF SPAIN AND PORTUGAL, COLLECTED BY KURT SCHINDLER, © 1941 HISPANIC INSTITUTE IN THE UNITED STATES. USED BY PERMISSION OF COLUMBIA UNIVERSITY, DEPARTMENT OF SPANISH AND PORTUGUESE.

There's a fi - es - ta to - day, tra la la la,_____

Gui - tars are be - gin - ning to play, tra la la la,_____

Sweet - ly their mu - sic rings out, tra la la la,_____

As ev - 'ry - one gath - ers a - bout, tra la la la.

Cas - ta - nets start keep-ing the beat, Danc - ers be - gin mov-ing their feet,

Whirl - ing a - way while ev - 'ry-one cries out "O - lé!"

For percussion parts, see p. 225.

Section A

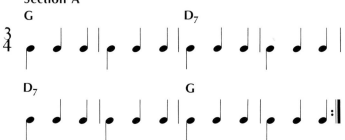

More About Tone Color   27

The Autoharp

This song has three sections—A, B, and C. Sections A and B use three Autoharp chords—G, D₇, and C. In section C the F chord is added.

Practice playing an Autoharp accompaniment for one of the sections. The letter names in the music will tell you when to change chords.

TAKE ME HOME, COUNTRY ROADS

WORDS AND MUSIC BY BILL DANOFF, TAFFY NIVERT, AND JOHN DENVER

1. Al - most Heav - en,___ West Vir - gin - ia,
2. All my mem - 'ries___ gath - er 'round___ her,

Blue Ridge Moun - tains, Shen - an - do - ah Riv - er.
Min - er's la - dy, strang - er to blue wa - ters.

Life is old___ there, old - er than the trees,___
Dark and dus - ty paint - ed on the sky.___

Young - er than the moun - tains, grow - ing like a breeze.___
Mis - ty rays of moon - shine, tear - drop in my eye.___

Coun - try roads,_____ take me home _____

The Recorder

If you have never played the soprano recorder before, practice these notes.

When you can play the notes B, A, and G on the soprano recorder, you will be able to play a countermelody for each song on pages 30 and 31.

Your recorder notes look like this.

Your fingers should cover these holes.

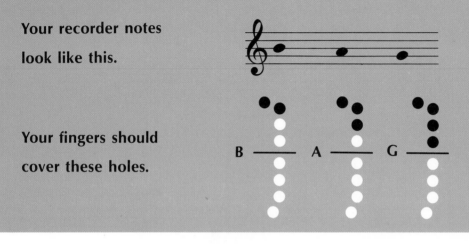

MY DAME HATH A LAME, TAME CRANE   ROUND

My dame hath a lame, tame crane,

My dame hath a crane that is lame.

Pray, gen-tle Jane, let my dame's lame, tame

crane Feed and come home a-gain.

Here are two countermelodies for "My Dame Hath a Lame,
Tame Crane." Choose one and play it all through the song.

Soprano recorder

TAKE TIME IN LIFE   FOLK SONG FROM LIBERIA

FROM AFRICAN SONGS © 1958 LYNN ROHRBOUGH.   USED BY PERMISSION WORLD AROUND SONGS. BURNSVILLE, N. C., U. S. A.

1. 2. I was pass - ing by, my broth-er / sis-ter called me in, And he / she said to

me, "You bet - ter take time in life." Peo - ple, take time in life, Peo - ple,

take time in life, Peo-ple, take time in life, 'cause you got far way to go.

Play this countermelody as others sing the melody of "Take
Time in Life."

Soprano recorder

The Guitar

The guitar has never been more popular nor used more widely than it is today.

This page introduces you to an easy way to play the C and G_7 chords on the guitar. The photographs and diagrams will help you learn how to play each chord.

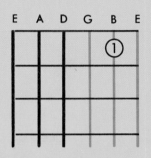

To play the C chord, put finger 1 (your index finger) on the B string. Strum the strings shown in red.

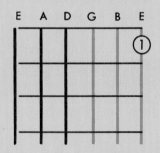

To play the G_7 chord, move finger 1 to the high-E string and strum the strings shown in red.

When you can change from the C chord to the G₇ chord easily,
play a guitar accompaniment as others sing this song. The
diagrams and letter names in the music will tell you when to
change from one chord to the other.

CHUMBARA

FRENCH-CANADIAN FOLK SONG

Chum - ba - ra, _____ chum - ba - ra chum - ba - ra, _____ chum - ba - ra

chum - ba - ra, _____ chum - ba - ra chum,chum,chum,chum,chum,chum,chum,chum,

Chum - ba - ra, _____ chum - ba - ra chum - ba - ra, _____ chum - ba - ra

chum - ba - ra, _____ chum - ba - ra chum, chum!

2. **Fy-do-lee**

3. **Chow-ber-ski**

4. **Chug-ah-lee**

5. **Say-too-mee**

6. **Boom-ta-da**

7. **Zow-lee-ski**

For further experience with playing the guitar, see p. 189.

More About Tone Color 33

The Guitar

PUTTIN' ON THE STYLE

AMERICAN FOLK SONG   NEW WORDS AND NEW MUSIC ADAPTATION BY NORMAN CAZDEN

Put - tin' on the ag - o - ny, put - tin' on the style,

That's what all the young folks are do - in' all the while. And

as I look a - round me, I'm ver - y apt to smile To

see so man - y peo - ple put - tin' on the style.

1. Young man in a car - riage,____ driv - in' like____ he's mad,
2. Sweet six - teen____ goes to school just____ to see the boys,
3. Young man home from col - lege____ makes____ a great dis - play,

With a pair of hors - es____ he bor-rowed from his dad; He
Turns and laughs and gig - gles____ at ev - 'ry lit - tle noise; She
With a fan - cy ad - jec - tive that he can hard - ly say; It

cracks his whip so live - ly just to watch his la - dy smile,____
turns this way a lit - tle, then____ turns that way a - while, But
can't be found in Web - ster's, and it won't be for a - while, But

34 More About Tone Color

But she knows he's on — ly put - tin' on the style.
we know that she's on — ly put - tin' on the style.
ev - 'ry - bod - y knows___ he's put - tin' on the style.

LA SINDA

FOLK SONG FROM SPAIN   COLLECTED BY J. DE JUAN   ENGLISH VERSION BY AURA KONTRA

COPYRIGHT © 1960 BY UNION MUSICAL ESPANOLA, MADRID. USED BY PERMISSION.

Here she comes with eyes beam-ing bright - ly, a rose in her hair,___
Spread the news to friends and com - pan - ions, for now is our chance,___

___ Here she comes with long skirts a - fly - ing, a scarf in her hand.
___ Hur - ry, we will meet in the vil - lage, she's read - y to dance.

Oh, la Sin - da___ claps her hands to the beat,

Oh, la Sin - da ___ taps her heels and her feet.
Sin - da,___

Oh, la Sin - da,___ danc - ing Sin - da, see her

danc - ing ___ in the street.

For percussion parts, see p. 224.

More About Tone Color 35

The Piano
GERMAN DANCE
ATTRIBUTED TO LUDWIG VAN BEETHOVEN

SECONDO
(LOW PART)

If you play the piano, practice one of the parts of *German Dance.* Then find someone to play the other part with you.

GERMAN DANCE

ATTRIBUTED TO LUDWIG VAN BEETHOVEN

PRIMO
(HIGH PART)

Instruments of the Orchestra

Listen to a recording that uses the tone color of orchestral instruments. You will hear some of the instruments of the brass, woodwind, and string families. Which of the instruments listed below are used in "Laughter Makes the World Go Round"?

flute	trumpet	violin
bassoon	tuba	cello
oboe	French horn	string bass
clarinet	trombone	viola

Here is the melody of "Laughter Makes the World Go Round" written for voices and instruments of the string, woodwind, and brass families. If you play one of these instruments, practice the round to play with the recording.

LAUGHTER MAKES THE WORLD GO ROUND

WORDS AND MUSIC BY JOHN WILSON

Laugh - ter makes the world go round, so the wise men say.

Laugh - ter is the rec - i - pe to make us all feel gay:

Ha, ha, ha, ha, ha, ha, ha, ha, ho, ho, ho, ho, ho, ho, ho.

Cello and Trombone

Clarinet and Trumpet

Organize an ensemble to sing and play "Laughter Makes the World Go Round." Plan your performance. Will you perform the piece in unison? As a two- or three-part round? Will the instruments, or voices, begin? Will the voices and instruments perform together? Think of other ways to combine tone colors.

CALL CHART 2: Orchestral Instruments. ⊚

Follow the call chart to help you hear how three families of instruments are used in a piece for orchestra.

Handel: *Water Music Suite,* "Allegro deciso"

---

1 CONTRAST OF STRINGS AND BRASS

---

2 STRINGS AND WOODWINDS TOGETHER

---

3 STRINGS ALONE

---

4 CONTRAST OF STRINGS AND BRASS

String Instruments

Listen for the tone color of string instruments on this recording.

🎵 Eddleman: *Shuffling Strings*

If you play the violin or cello, practice the part. When you are ready, play your part with the ensemble on the recording.

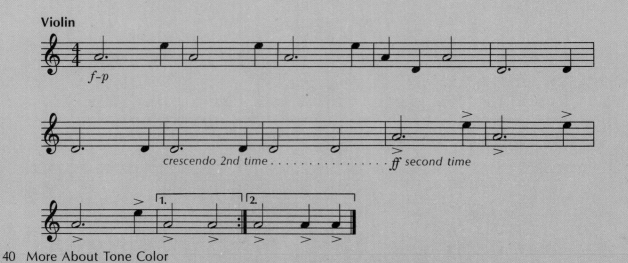

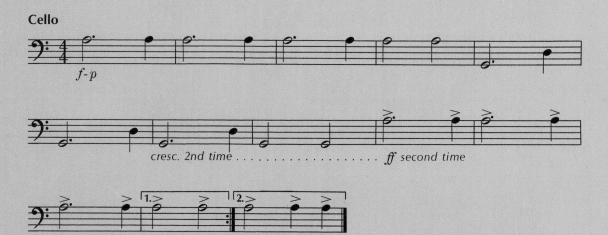

Brass Instruments

You have heard the tone color of string instruments playing in
ensemble. Now listen for the tone color of brass instruments on
this recording.

2 Eddleman: *Swingin' on the Levee*

If you play the trumpet or trombone, practice the part. Then
play along with the brass ensemble on the recording.

Trombone

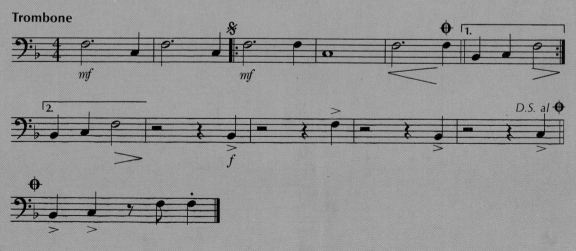

Woodwinds

Listen to the tone color of woodwind instruments on this recording.

🔘
2 Eddleman: *Latin Woods*

If you play the flute or clarinet, practice the part so you can play along with the ensemble on the recording.

Flute

Clarinet

Koto from Japan

Different Instruments from Different Cultures

Listen to the tone of some instruments
used by people from different cultures.
How many sounds can you identify?

● *Folk Instrument Collage*

Mbira from Africa

Steel drums from Trinidad

Ipu from Hawaii

Pipe from China

Dulcimer from the United States

Drums from Haiti

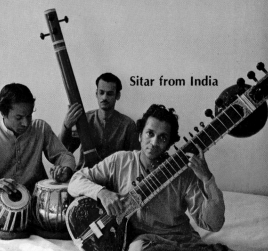

Sitar from India

WHAT DO YOU HEAR? 1: Various Tone Colors 🔘2

Can you hear tone color in music? Listen to these pieces. Each
time a number is called, decide which answer is correct.
Sometimes you may discover that more than one answer must
be chosen. Listen. Then choose your answer.

1	**2**	**3**
keyboard	keyboard	keyboard
electronic sound	electronic sound	electronic sound
folk instrument	folk instrument	folk instrument
voice	voice	voice
natural sound	natural sound	natural sound
recorder	recorder	recorder

4	**5**	**6**
keyboard	keyboard	keyboard
electronic sound	electronic sound	electronic sound
folk instrument	folk instrument	folk instrument
voice	voice	voice
natural sound	natural sound	natural sound
recorder	recorder	recorder

WHAT DO YOU HEAR? 2: Instruments of the Orchestra 🔘2

On this recording you will hear some of the instruments that
are used in the orchestra. Each time a number is called, decide
which answer is correct. Sometimes you may discover that more
than one answer is correct. Listen. Then choose your answer.

1	**2**	**3**
strings	strings	strings
woodwinds	woodwinds	woodwinds
brass	brass	brass
percussion	percussion	percussion

4	**5**	**6**
strings	strings	strings
woodwinds	woodwinds	woodwinds
brass	brass	brass
percussion	percussion	percussion

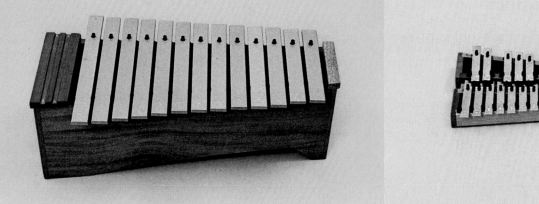

Pictured above are two of the instruments heard on the recording of "Carol from an Irish Cabin."

CAROL FROM AN IRISH CABIN
MUSIC BY DALE WOOD   WORDS ANONYMOUS

1. The cold wind blows o - ver the heath - er_____ The
2. The clean snow falls soft - ly, falls soft - ly,_____ The
3. So let there be no fear of dark - ness,_____ And

salt wind blows o - ver the sea,_____ The___
snow crys - tals cov - er the moor._____ Let___
let there be no fear of sea;_____ Let the

harsh wind blows down from the moun - tains,_____ And
wan - der - ers lost and grown wea - ry_____ Find
star guide the lost and for - sak - en_____ Safe

blows a white Christ - mas to me.
wel - come at my cab - in door.
o - ver the moor - lands to me.

More About Tone Color   49

Percussion

Add the tone color of percussion to this song from Trinidad.
Play the maracas throughout the song.

THE BABY BOY   CHRISTMAS SONG FROM TRINIDAD ⊙2

THE VIRGIN MARY HAD A BABY BOY FROM THE EDRIC CONNOR COLLECTION OF WEST INDIAN SPIRITUALS. COPYRIGHT 1945 BY BOOSEY & CO. LTD. RENEWED 1973.

1. The Vir - gin Mar - y had a ba - by boy, The
2. The an - gels sang___ for the ba - by boy, The
3. The Wise Men came to see the ba - by boy, The

Vir - gin Mar - y had a ba - by boy,   The Vir - gin Mar - y had a
an - gels sang___ for the ba - by boy,   The an - gels sang   for the
Wise Men came to see the ba - by boy,   The Wise Men came___ to see the

ba - by boy,___
ba - by boy,___   And they say that His name was Je - sus.
ba - by boy,___

He came___ from the glo - ry,   He came___ from the

Here are two other percussion parts to play throughout section B in "The Baby Boy." Notice the accent marks ($>$) in the bongo part.

Bongo

Claves

MUSIC OF THE NEAR EAST

Like people all over the world, the Near East people use music
for dancing and celebrations. The oboe and drum are often played to
celebrate holidays and weddings.

Here is some music for oboe and drum that comes from the central part of
Turkey where many people are farmers. In this music, the drummer hits the
left side of the drum with a small stick and the right side with a wooden
hammer.

Play along with the drummer. He plays the same rhythm pattern over and
over.

◉ *Turkish Oboe and Drum Dance Tune*

Here is a wedding song from Afghanistan. It is sung by two women. First they
sing about the new gold jewelry the bride wears in her hair. Then they sing
about the bride and groom.

◉ *Woman's Wedding Song*

Although there are some Christians and Jews who live in the Near East, most
Near Easterners believe in the religion called *Islam*. These people are called
Muslims. They believe that to be a good Muslim they must do at least four
important things. *1.* Give charity to the poor. *2.* Make a pledge of allegiance
to Islam. *3.* Observe a special period (one month each year) by eating only
after sunset. *4.* Make a trip (a Haj) to the holy shrine of Islam in the city of
Mecca, Arabia.

The next song comes from the town of Jaffa, Israel. It is about a trip to the holy
shrine of Islam. Notice that the song is sung as a solo (call) and response
(chorus). In some American churches people sing their hymns this way.

Keep time to the music by playing the drum part or by clapping your hands.

◉ *Song for the Haj*

Another kind of Near Eastern music belonged only to kings and princes who
hired poets and musicians to entertain in court. These poets and musicians
developed a special kind of music called *classical,* or *court* music.

Here is an example of classical, or court, music from Iran. It is performed by a
solo singer and a violinist. You will hear that the music begins softly in a low
register and ends loud in a high register.

◉ *Persian Classical Song with Violin*

Listen to the song again to discover why this Near Eastern music is said to have "free rhythm." Also, notice how the singer decorates the melody. This is called *ornamentation*.

The Near East is a very big area with many different landscapes, many kinds of people, and many kinds of music. You can almost compare the Near East to a jigsaw puzzle. The pieces are all of different size, shape, and color, but when you put them together they make sense as a whole.

SECTION 2: MELODY

INTRODUCTION TO MELODY

When you think of music, you are likely to think of melody—a series of tones related to each other that forms a line of sounds we *hear*.

In dance, line is *seen*. Sometimes when a dancer's body is still, your eyes see the line made by its position—from tip of toes to tip of fingers.

At other times, you see a moving line as the dancers' bodies move in space.

In poems, words are arranged into lines we *read*—a set of words
followed by another, then another. Some poems have long lines,
some very short lines. Other poems have a combination of long
and short lines.

THE NIGHT WILL NEVER STAY

The night will never stay,
The night will still go by,
Though with a million stars
You pin it to the sky;

Though you bind it with the blowing wind
And buckle it with the moon,
The night will slip away
Like sorrow or a tune.

Eleanor Farjeon

NIGHT

Stars over snow,
   And in the west a planet
Swinging below a star—
   Look for a lovely thing and
     you will find it,
It is not far—
It never will be far.

Sara Teasdale

PIET MONDRIAN: OPPOSITION OF LINES: RED AND YELLOW. PHILADELPHIA MUSEUM OF ART: THE A. E. GALLATIN COLLECTION.

In paintings, sometimes only
straight lines are used, carefully
placed to work against each
other and with each other,
giving a feeling of movement
and stillness together. Nothing
really moves, but our *eyes*
and our *minds* make us feel
movement.

Introduction to Melody 55

USING WHAT YOU KNOW ABOUT MELODY

Phrases/Melody Contour

This song has two sections—A and B. Which section has both short phrases and long phrases?

As you listen to the recording, follow the notation to discover the contour, or shape, of the melody in each phrase.

ANTHONY MAYBERRY WORDS AND MUSIC BY PATRICK P. ADAMS

© 1972 BY POPDRAW MUSIC CORP., NEW YORK, NEW YORK

1. An - tho - ny May - ber - ry ran a - way quite ear - ly
2. An - tho - ny May - ber - ry seemed ver - y sad as he

yes - ter - day___ af - ter - noon.   With a dime in his hand,
turned to look back one last time.   With a tear in his eye,

want - ed to be a man, car - ried his clothes on a broom.___
An - tho - ny said good-by, head - ed toward Ma - ple and Vine.___

B REFRAIN

But, An - tho - ny,___ tell me where will you sleep?   And,

But, An - th'ny, where will you sleep?

56 Using What You Know About Melody

An - tho - ny, _____ tell me what will you eat? _____ Re -

An - th'ny, what will you eat?

mem - ber _____ where the shoes on your feet come from. _____

And where will your shoes come from? _____

THE WINDOWS OF THE WORLD

WORDS AND MUSIC BY BURT BACHARACH AND HAL DAVID

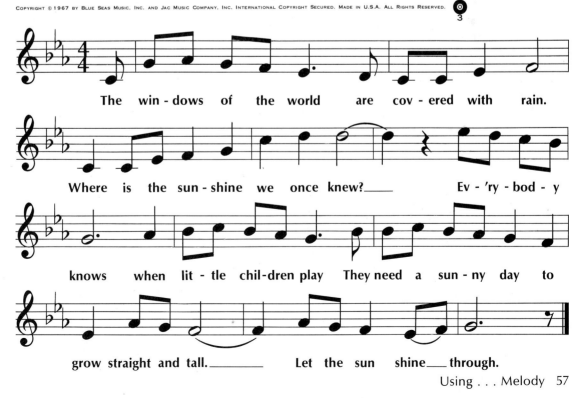

The win - dows of the world are cov - ered with rain.

Where is the sun - shine we once knew? _____ Ev - 'ry - bod - y

knows when lit - tle chil - dren play They need a sun - ny day to

grow straight and tall. _____ Let the sun shine _____ through.

Using . . . Melody 57

Steps, Leaps, Repeats

Listen to the recording of "Everybody's Got a Song." Follow the notation to find where the tones of the melody repeat, where they move by step, and where they leap.

EVERYBODY'S GOT A SONG

WORDS AND MUSIC BY BARBERI PAULL

© 1979 BARBERI PAULL. USED BY PERMISSION.

It was just a ___ sim - ple lit - tle mel - o - dy, ___ I used to ___ lis-

- ten to it sing to ___ me. ___ It al - ways ___ came ___ to keep me com - pa - ny, ___

___ And it would help me through when ___ ev - 'ry - thing was go - ing ___ wrong.
All those times when noth - ing seems to go my ___ way,

___ Some - times I ___ e - ven got to sing a - long. ___ I came to ___ rec-
___ No - bod - y ___ cares ___ a - bout a thing I ___ say, ___ I set - tle ___ back

- og - nize it as my ___ own, ___ my own ___ song.
___ and lis - ten. Come on, ___ song, ___ sing a - way. ___

Ev - 'ry - bod - y, ___

ev - 'ry - bod - y, ___ ev - 'ry - bod - y, ev - 'ry - bod - y's got his own song.
her

58 Using . . . Melody

Ev - 'ry - bod - y's___ got his/her own song. Ev -'ry-bod-y's got his/her own song.

Ev - 'ry - bod - y,___ ev - 'ry - bod - y's___ got his/her own___ song.

1. Do do do do do do,___ lis-ten to it, sing a - long._____

2. lis-ten to it sing a - long.___

_____ Do do do do do do,___ lis-ten to it, sing a - long!___ Do do___ do.___

Before listening to the recording of "Lonesome Valley," take
time to notice where tones repeat, where they move upward or
downward by step and by leap.

For a recorder countermelody, see p. 211.

LONESOME VALLEY
FOLK HYMN

You must walk ___ that lone-some val - ley, ___ You have to walk___

___ it by your-self,___ No - bod - y else___ can walk it

for you,___ You have to walk ___ it all a - lone. ___

Using . . . Melody 59

Comparing Two Melodies

A ballad tells a story in song. Here are two versions of the same ballad. Listen to both versions on the recordings and notice the difference between the two melodies.

THE GOLDEN VANITY

FOLK SONG FROM ENGLAND

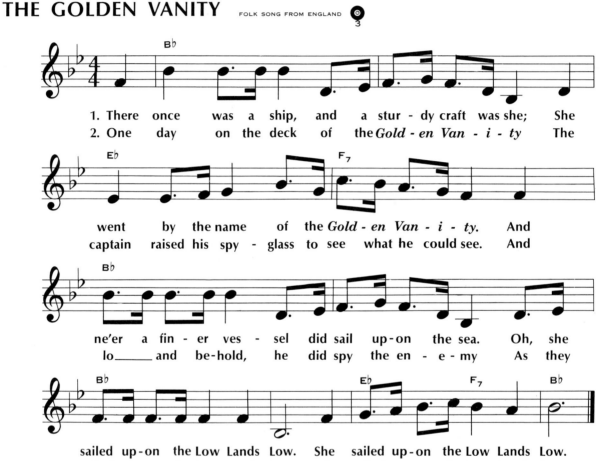

1. There once was a ship, and a stur - dy craft was she; She
2. One day on the deck of the *Gold - en Van - i - ty* The

went by the name of the *Gold - en Van - i - ty.* And
captain raised his spy - glass to see what he could see. And

ne'er a fin - er ves - sel did sail up - on the sea. Oh, she
lo____ and be - hold, he did spy the en - e - my As they

sailed up - on the Low Lands Low. She sailed up - on the Low Lands Low.
sailed up - on the Low Lands Low. As they sailed up - on the Low Lands Low.

3. The captain was pond'ring the course he would pursue,
   When up spoke the cabin boy, the youngest of the crew.
   "Pray, sir, what will you give me to rout the foe for you
   As they sail upon the Low Lands Low?" (*2 times*)

4. The captain was amazed and a little bit annoyed
   To think he must depend on a lowly cabin boy,
   But he said he'd give his daughter, his very pride and joy,
   If he'd sink them in the Low Lands Low. (*2 times*)

5. The boy spread his arms and into the sea he dived.
   He swam and he swam, it's a wonder he survived!
   He bored some tiny holes in the other vessel's side
   And he sank it in the Low Lands Low. (*2 times*)

6. Then back once again to the *Vanity* he sped.
   He thought as he swam of the pretty girl he'd wed,
   For, "You shall have my daughter," the captain'd plainly said,
   "And you'll sail upon the Low Lands Low." (*2 times*)

7. And when he reached the ship and was safely at her side,
   "Good captain, help me come aboard!" the cabin boy did cry.
   The captain, though, ignored him, and merely breathed a sigh
   As he sailed upon the Low Lands Low." (*2 times*)

8. "Good captain, help me up," cried the cabin boy once more,
   "Or else I'll bore your ship and send it to the ocean floor."
   The captain then moved quickly and pulled the lad aboard
   And they sailed upon the Low Lands Low." (*2 times*)

THE TURKISH REVERY
AMERICAN FOLK SONG

1. "Cap-tain, cap-tain, ___ What will you give me If
2. "Gold and sil-ver ___ Shin - ing so bright, And my

I do sink the ___ *Turk-ish Rev-er-y,* If I sink her in the low-down,
fair-est daugh-ter shall wed ___ you to-night, If you sink her in the low-down,

low - down, ___ low - down, If I sink her in the low-down lone-some low?"
low - down, ___ low - down, If you sink her in the low-down lone-some low!"

Using . . . Melody 61

3. Then he bared his breast
   And he swam in the tide,
   And he bored three holes in the old ship's side,
   And he sank her in the low-down, low-down, low-down,
   And he sank her in the low-down lonesome low.

4. Then he bared his breast
   And he swam in the tide,
   He swam till he came to his own ship's side
   As she rolled in the low-down, . . .

5. "Captain, captain,
   Take me on board!
   If you don't, you'll have to forfeit your word,
   For you promised in the low-down, . . ."

6. "Sailor boy, sailor boy,
   Don't appeal to me,
   For you drowned sixty souls when you sank the *Revery*,
   When you sank her in the low-down, . . ."

7. "If it weren't for the love
   That I bear for your men,
   I'd sink you the same as I sank them!
   I'd sink you in the low-down, . . ."

8. Then he bared his breast
   And down swam he.
   He swam till he came to the bottom of the sea,
   And he drowned in the low-down, . . .

Now compare the two versions by answering some of these questions.

1. In which melody are all the phrases the same length? In which melody do you find both long and short phrases?

2. In which melody do you find two phrases that are similar?

3. Find the lowest and highest note in each melody. Which version has the wider range?

4. In which melody do you find an octave leap?

5. Which melody is major? Which is minor?

Melody Contour

Here are the beginnings of three patriotic songs that you know. Can you name each song by looking at the melody contour (general shape) of the first phrase?

CALL CHART 3: Steps and Leaps

Listen to a melody that is used in a piece by Bach. Can you hear when the tones move mostly by step and when they move mostly by leap?

Bach: *Two-Part Invention,* No. 6, Version I

1 Mostly by step		**5** Mostly by step	
2 Mostly by leap		**6** Mostly by leap	
3 Mostly by step		**7** Mostly by step	
4 Mostly by leap		**8** Mostly by leap	

Follow the chart again as you listen to this melody and a countermelody working together. Notice how the melody and countermelody move in opposite directions.   Bach: *Two-Part Invention,* No. 6, Version 2

Melody Contour/Sequences

Listen to the recording of "People Take Care." Follow the contour, or shape, of the melody.

PEOPLE, TAKE CARE

TRADITIONAL WORDS   MUSIC BY ANTHONY DONATO

FROM MODERN CANONS, EDITED BY HERMAN REICHENBACH. COPYRIGHT 1948 MERCURY MUSIC, INC. USED BY PERMISSION.

Peo - ple who live, peo - ple who live, peo - ple who live in glass hous-es,

Peo - ple liv - ing in glass hous - es should not throw, should not throw,

Peo - ple liv - ing in glass hous - es should not, should not throw stones.

"By the Waters of Babylon" has melody ideas that are heard again at different pitch levels. These are called *sequences*.

BY THE WATERS OF BABYLON

MUSIC BY PHILIP HAYES

By _____ the wa - ters, the wa - ters of Bab - y - lon

We sat down and wept, ___ yea wept, ___ yea wept _____ When

we re - mem-bered thee, re - mem-bered thee _____ O __ Zi - on.

There we hang our harps, hang our harps, hang our harps on the wil - lows.

Listen to hear how sequences are used in a piece by Handel.

◎₃ Handel: *Royal Fireworks Suite,* "Minuetto"

CALL CHART 4: Melody Contour ◎₃

Listen to these pieces to hear how steps, leaps, repeated tones, and sequences are used to create melody contours.

Hill: *The Bird Fancyer's Delight* (excerpts)

1 Repeats, leaps, sequences	
	Tune for Woodlark
2 Steps, repeats, leaps, sequences	
	Tune for Bullfinch
3 Mostly leaps, sequences	
	Tune for Canary, 1
4 Mostly steps, no sequences	
	Tune for Woodlark
5 Steps, repeats, leaps, sequences	
	Tune for Parrot

WHAT DO YOU HEAR? 3: Sequences ◎₃

Listen for sequences or no sequences in these pieces. Each time a number is called, decide which answer is correct.

1 SEQUENCES		NO SEQUENCES
		Handel: *Minuetto*
2 SEQUENCES		NO SEQUENCES
		Hahvah nahgeela
3 SEQUENCES		NO SEQUENCES
		Eddleman: *Latin Woods*
4 SEQUENCES		NO SEQUENCES
		Strauss: *Also sprach Zarathustra*
5 SEQUENCES		NO SEQUENCES
		Hill: *Tune for Bullfinch*

EXPERIENCING THE ARTS:
The Use of Space

A mobile is a special kind of visual art. What makes it different from painting, or sculpture, or architecture?

COLLECTION. THE MUSEUM OF MODERN ART, NEW YORK. COMMISSIONED BY THE ADVISORY COMMITTEE FOR THE STAIRWELL OF THE MUSEUM.

A painting, such as this very famous one, is on a flat canvas. How does it give us a feeling of space?

How does architecture use space differently from a mobile or a painting?

In dance, space is used in a special way. What makes dance something like a mobile? In what way is dance different from a mobile? Different from a painting? Different from architecture?

Music can give a sense of space, but it does it differently from any art you see with your eyes.

A melody has a "shape" that is heard. It can be played at different levels—high, medium, or low registers. This gives a feeling of space, using *musical* space.

Follow this chart as you listen to melodies played in different registers, using musical space.

CALL CHART 5: Register ⊚

Britten: *Simple Symphony*, Movement 2

1 Melody 1 repeated in same and different registers—use of sequence

2 Melody 2 in medium register; accompaniment in low register

3 Melody 2 in low register; accompaniment in high register

4 Melody 1 repeated in same and different registers—use of sequence

5 Melody 2 in medium register; accompaniment in low register

In music, space is not something you see, as in the visual arts and dance. It is something felt, as you hear sounds at different levels of high and low. There is no real space among the sounds, but it can feel as if there is.

Each of these arts uses space in its own way, and each way has something different about it. Every art has its special way to add to your experience.

WHAT PEOPLE DO WITH MUSIC: Listen

As you sing this song with the recording, think about this question: Where are the sounds coming from?

For a percussion ensemble, see p. 228.

ORION

WORDS AND MUSIC BY JAMES ZIMMERMAN

© 1972 JAMES ZIMMERMAN

1. O - ri - on is a - ris - ing, You can see his stars a - blaz-
2. The day is get - ting cold - er, And I real - ly start to won-

- ing in the mid - dle of a clear - eyed coun - try sky.
- der why we're cloud - ing all the coun - try skies to gray.

And it's nev - er too sur - pris - ing that the sky is still a - maz-
The world is get - ting old - er, You can hear it in the thun-

- ing way out here where noth - ing hides it from my eyes.
- der and the rain might come and chase us all a - way.

And sleep - ing out - side in a bag as a

kid, It seems like the best thing that I ev - er did; And

chas - ing the shad - ows and the tracks in the snow, don't you

This time, listen to the recording without singing. Get your mind involved in hearing what the music does. For each of the five elements listed below, choose the qualities you hear.

1. TONE COLOR: man's voice—clarinet—children's voices—guitar—piano

2. RHYTHM: meter in 3—meter in 4—change in meter—little syncopation—much syncopation

3. MELODY: all long phrases—all short phrases—both long and short phrases

4. HARMONY (TEXTURE): melody alone—melody with chords—melody with countermelody

5. FORM: ABCD—ABAB with coda (ending section)

WHAT HAPPENS
WHEN YOU LISTEN TO MUSIC?

Sounds
come from your own
performance, records,
tapes, radio, television,
concerts or ANYWHERE.

Are received
by ear drum that
is sensitive to sound
vibrations

Mind perceives
qualities of sound movement
created by melody, rhythm,
harmony, tone color, form.

Feelings react
to all things the music is doing.

Each person reacts to the same
music, but in different ways
because of differences in
the way each person feels.

Judgment is made
about how musical qualities
are used, and how the whole
piece makes you feel.

MORE ABOUT MELODY

Melodies that Outline Chords

Some melodies use the tones that outline a chord. The melody of "Morning Has Broken" uses the tones of the C chord in both an upward and a downward direction.

Find these patterns in the melody. Play them on the bells.

MORNING HAS BROKEN
TRADITIONAL GAELIC MELODY   WORDS BY ELEANOR FARJEON

WORDS REPRINTED BY PERMISSION OF HAROLD OBER ASSOCIATES, INC. COPYRIGHT © 1957 ELEANOR FARJEON.

1. Morn-ing has bro - ken   Like the first morn - ing,   Black-bird has
2. Sweet the rain's new   fall   Sun - lit from heav - en,   Like the first

spo - ken   Like   the   first bird._____   Praise   for   the
dew - fall   on   the   first grass._____   Praise   for   the

sing - ing!   Praise   for   the   morn - ing!   Praise   for   them,
sweet - ness   of   the   wet   gar - den,   Sprung   in   com -

spring - ing   Fresh   from   the   Word!_____
plete - ness.   Where   His   feet   pass. _____

The countermelody for "Morning Has Broken" on page 75 has a contour, or shape, that is different from that of the melody.

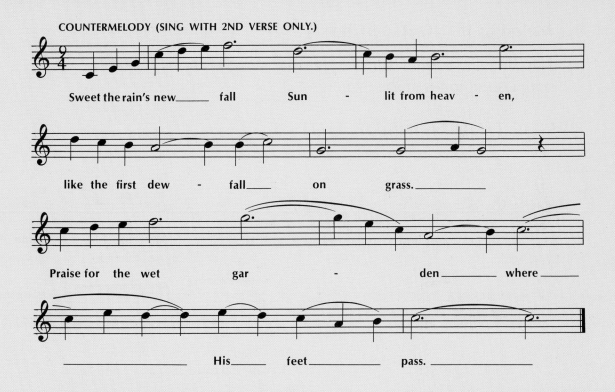

COUNTERMELODY (SING WITH 2ND VERSE ONLY.)

Sweet the rain's new___ fall   Sun - lit from heav - en,

like the first dew - fall___ on   grass.___

Praise for the wet   gar - den___ where___

___ His___ feet___ pass.___

BREAD FOR THE WORLD

1. Praise and thanksgiving,
   Father, we offer,
   for all things living
      thou madest good;
         harvest of sown fields,
         fruits of the orchard,
         hay from the mown fields,
            blossom and wood.

2. Bless thou the labor
   we bring to serve thee,
   that with our neighbor
      we may be fed.
         Sowing or tilling,
         we would work with thee;
         harvesting, milling,
            for daily bread.

3. Father, providing
   food for thy children,
   thy wisdom guiding
      teaches us share
         one with another,
         so that rejoicing
         with us, our brother
            may know thy care.

4. Then will thy blessing
   reach every people;
   all men confessing
      thy gracious hand.
         Where thy will reigneth
         no man will hunger;
         thy love sustaineth;
            fruitful the land.

Albert F. Bayly
Copyright Albert F. Bayly. Reprinted by permission.

More About Melody 75

Melodies that Outline Chords

Find the places in the B section of this song where the melody outlines the tones of the F chord—F A C.

UPSIDE DOWN–INSIDE OUT

WORDS AND MUSIC BY PHIL NAMANWORTH AND JOEY LEVINE

© Copyright 1977 Crushing Music (BMI) and Shirdi Music (ASCAP) Used by permission.

1. Ev - 'ry - bod - y knows a friend can be___ good
face,   more than an - y -

com - pa - ny,___   No - bod - y's clos - er to me___
bod - y else,___   I can al - ways see___ my - self___

than you.   'Cause you're the kind of friend who's
in you.   It makes me wan - na smile to

al - ways there___ on rain - y days,___   Think - in' up so
know that I___ was all a - lone,___   Now I have a

ma - ny ways___   To help me through.___
chap - er - one,___   Guess who?___

When I'm feel - ing up - side down,   in - side out,

Stars fall - in' from my skies.   You can turn my

seams a - round, Put my toes back on the ground,—

with just the love — in your eyes.— 2. Hey there, fun-ny

— in your eyes.—

Scales

The tones of a melody can be organized in several ways.

To discover one organization of tones, start anywhere on the piano keyboard and play half steps (don't skip any black or white keys) in a downward direction, then in an upward direction.

Arrange the bells in half steps from the lowest C to the C above and play them one after the other upward and downward.

What you have played and heard, using an organization of tones in half steps, is called a *chromatic scale*.

Now listen for places in this music where the tones move downward by half steps.

 Mozart: *String Quartet in D Minor*, Movement 4

For another organization of tones, arrange the bells in whole steps. Put the bells in this order—C-D-E-F$^\#$-G$^\#$-A$^\#$-C and play them one after the other from low C to the C above, then downward. You will be playing an arrangement of tones called a *whole-tone* scale.

Listen for the special sound of a whole-tone scale in this recording of a familiar tune.

 America in Whole Tone

More About Melody 77

The Major Scale

Half steps and whole steps may be arranged in a variety of ways. Many of the songs you sing and the pieces you listen to use an organization of whole steps and half steps that is called a *major scale.*

Arrange the bells to play a major scale, starting on G. Notice the arrangement of whole steps and half steps. Play this major scale upward and downward to hear its special sound.

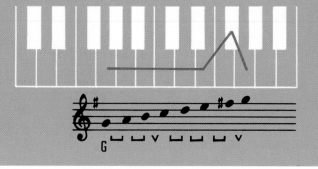

For percussion parts, see p. 227.

GONNA BUILD A MOUNTAIN

WORDS AND MUSIC BY LESLIE BRICUSSE AND ANTHONY NEWLEY

FROM THE MUSICAL PRODUCTION "STOP THE WORLD—I WANT TO GET OFF"   © COPYRIGHT 1961 TRO ESSEX MUSIC LTD., LONDON, ENGLAND
TRO—LUDLOW MUSIC, INC., New York, controls all publication rights to the USA and Canada. Used by permission.

Gon-na build a moun-tain From a lit-tle hill.

Gon-na build a moun-tain, Least I hope I will.

Gon-na build a moun-tain, Gon-na build it high.

I don't know how I'm gon-na do it, On-ly know I'm gon-na try.

The Minor Scale

Some songs you sing and pieces you listen to are based on an organization of whole steps and half steps that is called a *minor scale.*

Arrange the bells to play a minor scale, starting on G. Notice the arrangement of whole steps and half steps. Play this minor scale upward and downward to hear its special sound.

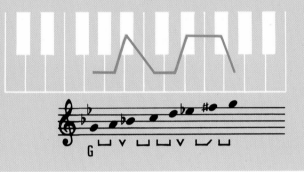

GO DOWN, MOSES

BLACK SPIRITUAL

1. When Is - rael was in E - gypt's land, "Let my peo - ple go."
2. "Thus spoke the Lord," bold Mo - ses said, "Let my peo - ple go."

Op-pressed so hard they could not stand, "Let my peo - ple go."
"If not I'll smite your first - born dead." "Let my peo - ple go."

REFRAIN

Go down, Mo - ses, 'Way down in E - gypt land, ____

Tell ____ old Phar - aoh, "Let my peo - ple go."

Songs in Major or Minor

The Major Scale

"Everybody Loves Saturday Night" is based on a D-major scale. Notice that the arrangement of whole steps and half steps is the same as it is in the G-major scale shown on page 78 in your book. But this arrangement starts on the key tone D.

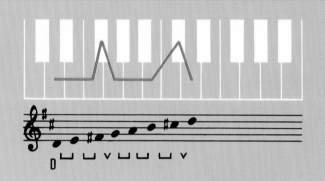

EVERYBODY LOVES SATURDAY NIGHT

FOLK SONG FROM GHANA

Ev - 'ry - bod - y loves Sat - ur - day night,

Ev - 'ry - bod - y loves Sat - ur - day night.

Ev - 'ry-bod - y, ev - 'ry-bod - y, ev - 'ry-bod - y, ev - 'ry-bod - y,

Ev - 'ry - bod - y loves Sat - ur - day night.

The Minor Scale

"Artsa alinu" is based on a D-minor scale. The arrangement of whole steps and half steps is different from the D-major scale shown on page 80 in your book.

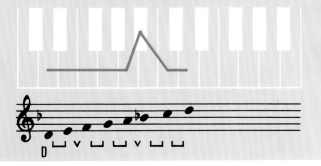

ARTSA ALINU

FOLK SONG FROM ISRAEL

For percussion parts, see p. 234.

VOICES AND INSTRUMENTS

La la la la la, la la la la la, La la la la la la.

La la la la la, la la la la la, La la la la la la.

La la la la, la la la la la la, La la la la,

la la la la la la, La la la la la la la;

La la la la la la la. La la la la la la la;

La la la la la la la.

Experiences with World Musics: India

One of the reasons the music of India sounds so different to us is that it is based on different organizations of tones. In the classical music of India, melodies are based on *ragas*.

A raga, like a scale, is an organized series of tones from which a musical composition is developed. There are hundreds of ragas, each having a particular name and structure.

On this recording, you will hear the sound of a familiar melody
as it is written in the Western major-scale system. Then you will
hear it as it is written based on two Indian ragas—first, raga
Bhairavi, then raga Purvi.

As you listen, notice how each organization of tones gives the
melody a special feeling.

🔘 *A Melody Three Ways*

1. Melody based on the major scale

2. Melody based on Raga Bhairavi

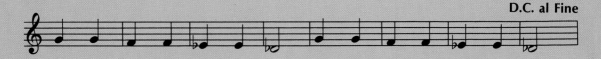

3. Melody based on Raga Purvi

The Pentatonic Scale

Folk music from many cultures is often based on a 5-tone scale called *pentatonic*. To hear the special sound of music that is based on a pentatonic scale, make up a melody on the black keys of the piano or on the upper row of the bells.

Before you begin, think about these questions. What meter will you use— $\frac{2}{4}$, $\frac{3}{4}$, $\frac{4}{4}$, or $\frac{6}{8}$? Will your melody move by steps, by leaps, by repeated tones, or by a combination of all three?

To add texture to your melody, choose someone to play (on the bells) one of the ostinato parts notated below. The meter of the bell part must match the meter of your melody.

With a mallet held in the left hand, play G♭ on notes with stems down. Play D♭ on notes with stems up.

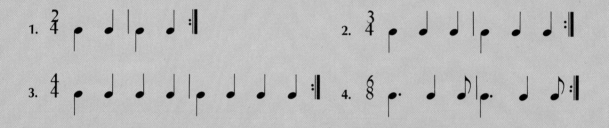

The song on page 85 is based on a pentatonic scale starting on F. Play the scale, upward and downward, to hear the general sound of "There's No Hidin' Place."

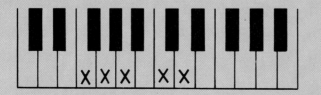

THERE'S NO HIDIN' PLACE

BLACK SPIRITUAL

There's no hid - in' place down there, There's no hid - in' place down there. Oh, I went to the rock to hide my face, The rock cried out, "No hid - in' place," There's no hid - in' place down there.

1. Oh, the rock cried, "I'm burn - in', too," Oh, the rock cried, "I'm burn - in', too"; Oh, the rock cried out, "I'm burn - in', too, I want to go to heav-en as well as you." There's no hid - in' place down there. 2. Oh, the

fox got a hole in the ground, Oh, the fox got a hole in the ground; Oh, the fox got a hole, the bird got a nest, But us___ poor___ sin-ners got no hidin' place. There's no hid - in' place down

1.
there.

2. Oh, the there. There's no hid - in' place down there, There's no hid - in' place down there. Oh, I went to the rock to hide my face, The rock cried out, "No hid - in' place," There's no hid - in' place down there.

Tonal Music

You have sung and played melodies based on a variety of scales—each scale focusing on one tone, the key tone.

Music that uses one scale at a time to organize the sound is called *tonal* music.

Using the four fingers of each hand, place your fingers on the keys that show the C scale in the diagram at the bottom of the page. Practice "playing" the C scale on the diagram, then try playing the C scale on the piano keyboard.

Look at the diagram at the bottom of page 87. It shows you how to play the D scale. Practice "playing" the D scale on the diagram, then try playing the D scale on the piano keyboard.

When you can play both scales, try playing the melody of "Chumbara" (page 33 in your book) in the key of C, then in the key of D.

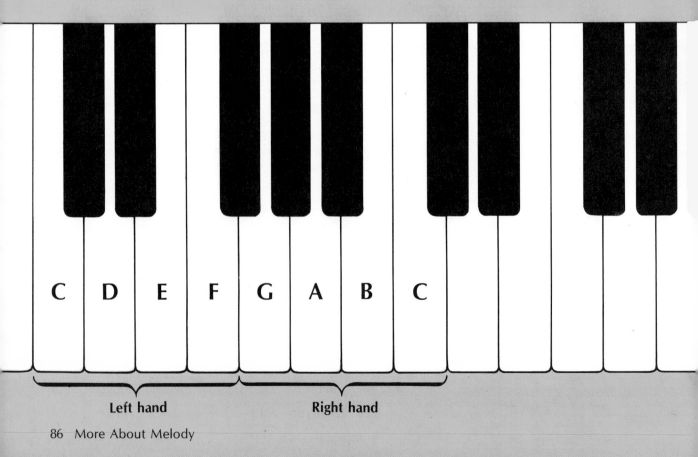

Left hand   Right hand

Polytonal Music

You have discovered that music that uses one scale at a time to organize its sound is called *tonal*. The key tone, or first note of the scale, gives a focus to the sound.

In some music, more than one scale is used *at the same time*. When music uses several scales together, it is called *polytonal*.

To hear the general sound of polytonal music, play "Chumbara" using the tones of the C scale. At the same time, ask someone else to play the same tune using the tones of the D scale.

Now, listen to a piano piece that is polytonal. Notice the special sound when two scales are used together.

 Starer: *Black and White*

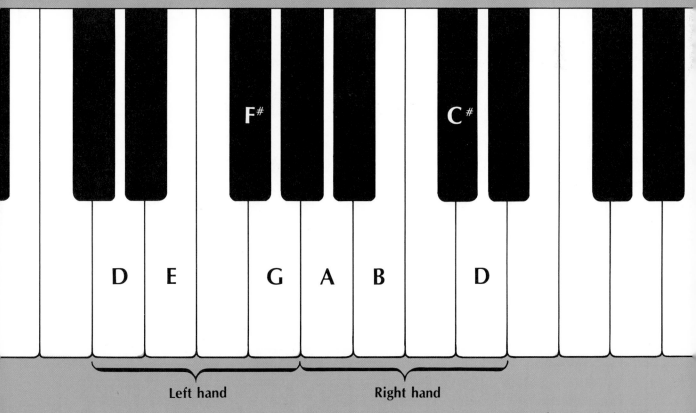

Left hand   Right hand

ATONAL MUSIC

Some music uses an organization of tones in which there is no one focus sound—no key tone. All the tones are of equal importance. This music is called *atonal.*

Many composers use all the tones within the octave as a basis for their music. The twelve tones are arranged in a certain order, called a *tone row.*

Listen to this atonal piece played by a woodwind quintet.

Eddleman: *Dualisms No. 2*

To play a tone row, arrange twelve bells in four sets of three bells as shown in the diagram at the bottom of pages 88 and 89.

After you have arranged the tone row, experiment to find ways of playing it.

1. Play the tones from left to right—the *original.* (You may repeat a tone several times when you get to it, but don't go back to it once you go on.)

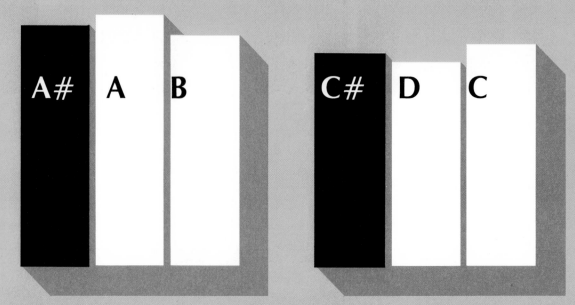

2. Play the row from right to left—the *retrograde*.

3. Play the tones in each set at the same time. Use three mallets, or strike them with the edge of a ruler or comb. Play the retrograde in the same way.

4. Going from left to right, play the tones in each set separately, then all three together. Play the retrograde in the same way.

After you have experimented with ways of playing the tone row, you can play along with the recording of *Dualisms 2*.

There are four places in the music where the instruments play a long sustained sound. Fill in one of the sustained sounds by playing the bells in one box of the tone row. During the next sustained sound, play the bells in a different box. Play another set of bells during the third sustained sound and the last set of bells during the fourth sustained sound.

Another time, play your part in a different way.

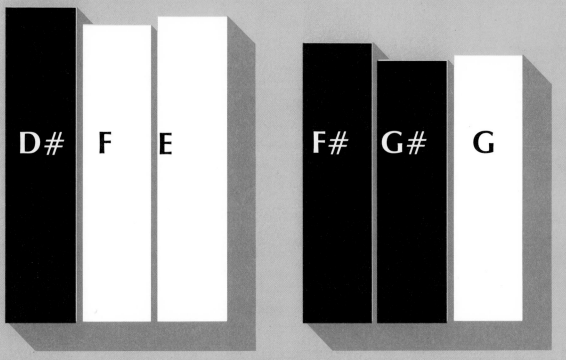

WHAT DO YOU HEAR? 4: Major and Minor Tonality

Listen to these pieces. Each time a number is called, choose the word that describes the tonality (the organization of whole and half steps). Is it major, or minor?

---

1 MAJOR   MINOR

Bach: *Two-Part Invention,* No. 6

---

2 MAJOR   MINOR

Mi Caballo Blanco

---

3 MAJOR   MINOR

Raindrops Keep Falling on My Head

---

4 MAJOR   MINOR

Ez Jahia Ez Dantza

This piece for orchestra has three sections. Each time a number is called, choose the word that describes the tonality.

---

1 MAJOR   MINOR

---

2 MAJOR   MINOR

---

3 MAJOR   MINOR

Tchaikovsky: *Dance of the Reed Flutes*

WHAT DO YOU HEAR? 5: Tonal, Atonal ⊚

Listen to the recording. Each time a number is called, choose the word that describes the tonality. Is the music tonal, or atonal? If it is tonal, decide whether the melody is built on a major or a minor scale.

1   TONAL   ATONAL
     major   minor

2   TONAL   ATONAL
     major   minor

3   TONAL   ATONAL
     major   minor

4   TONAL   ATONAL
     major   minor

5   TONAL   ATONAL
     major   minor

6   TONAL   ATONAL
     major   minor

Balkan Hills Schottische
Joshua Fought the Battle of Jericho
Hill: *Tune for Canary, 1*
Eddleman: *Dualisms, No. 2*
Starer: *Variants for Violin and Piano*
Mozart: *String Quartet in D Minor*, Movement 4

Tonality

Here is a Christmas carol from Spain. Listen to the recording and decide whether the tonality is minor, or major.

CAROL OF THE BIRDS

TRADITIONAL CAROL FROM SPAIN   ENGLISH WORDS BY ROSEMARY JACQUES

1. The night the Child was born,_____   The skies were bright as morn,   The
2. The crea-tures proud and tall,_____   The low-liest ones of all,   Did
3. And birds from ev-'ry-where_____   Flew gent-ly through the air   And

heav'ns were filled with won - ders;_____   There shone a ra-diant star;_____
jour-ney forth to Beth-le-hem;_____   And round the man-ger bed_____
hov-ered o'er the sta - ble;_____   The ea-gle and the quail_____

_____ It beck oned near and far, "Come__ ye, oh come and praise_____
_____ They hum-bly bowed their heads, For__they had come to praise_____
_____ The wren, the night-in-gale With__ one sweet voice did praise_____

Him."_____   There shone a ra-diant__ star;_____   It
Him._____   And round the man-ger__ bed_____   They
Him._____   The ea-gle and__ the__ quail,_____   The

beck-oned near and far, "Come__ ye, oh come and praise Him."_____
hum-bly bowed their heads, For__ they had come to praise Him._____
wren, the night-in-gale With__ one sweet voice did praise Him._____

Is this song based on a minor scale, or a major scale? What else
can you discover about each section of the song?

SWEET LITTLE JESUS BABY

CHRISTMAS SPIRITUAL   ENGLISH TEXT BY WALTER EHRET

Sweet lit - tle Je - sus ba - by in the hay,____

Just come from heav - en this - a Christ - mas day.____

Born in a sta - ble as the proph - ets say,____

Sweet lit - tle Je - sus ba - by in the hay.____

Lit - tle one,____ pure and ho - ly, Ma - ry's son,____

Born so low - ly in the cat - tle stall,____ Lord of all,____

babe so beau - ti - ful, sleep - ing peace - ful - ly.

Tonality

Is the tonality of this song major, or minor?

THE HURON CAROL

CHRISTMAS CAROL FROM CANADA   ENGLISH WORDS BY J. E. MIDDLETON

TEXT BY PERMISSION OF THE FREDERICK HARRIS MUSIC CO., LTD.

1. 'Twas in the moon of win-ter-time When all the birds had fled,
2. With-in a lodge of bro-ken bark The ten-der babe was found,

That might-y Git-chi Man-i-tou Sent an-gel choirs in-stead.
A rag-ged robe of rab-bit skin En-wrapped his beau-ty 'round;

Be-fore their light the stars grew dim, And won-d'ring hunt-ers heard the hymn:___
And as the hunt-er braves drew nigh The an-gel song rang loud and high:___

"Je - sus, your King, is born. Je - sus is born.

In ex - cel - sis glo - ri - a!"

3. The earliest moon of wintertime
   Is not so round and fair
   As was the ring of glory on
   The helpless infant there.
   The chiefs from far before him knelt
   With gifts of fox and beaver pelt.
   "Jesus, your King, is born.
   Jesus is born. *In excelsis gloria!*"

4. O children of the forest free,
   O sons of Manitou,
   The holy child of earth and heav'n
   Is born today for you.
   Come kneel before the radiant boy
   Who brings you beauty, peace, and joy.
   "Jesus, your King, is born.
   Jesus is born. *In excelsis gloria!*"

STYLES: PERFORMANCE

A melody can be performed in a variety of ways by changing the tonality, rhythm, tempo, dynamics, tone color, and texture. For some melodies, there is no one right way—no one "proper style." Each different style of performance has a musical flavor of its own.

"Amazing Grace" has been sung and played by many people since the early days of America. In this sound collage, you will hear the melody performed in different styles. The chart will help you hear what is going on in each performance.

CALL CHART 6: Styles of Performance ◉
5

1 Melody alone—played on a dulcimer

2 Melody ornamented—played on a dulcimer

3 Melody with a drone accompaniment—played on a dulcimer

4 Melody ornamented—sung by a woman with vocal accompaniment

5 Melody ornamented—played on a bagpipe with drone accompaniment

6 Melody sung by children with Autoharp and recorder accompaniment

7 Music performed by adult voices

8 Melody ornamented—sung by a woman with piano and organ accompaniment

In Call Chart 6 (page 95) you heard the "Amazing Grace" melody performed in various contrasting styles. You heard

- different vocal tone colors,
- different instrumental tone colors,
- different textures—combination of parts,
- different ways of performing the melody and rhythm.

Now, create your own style of performance by using the melody with some of the added parts on page 97.

AMAZING GRACE

EARLY AMERICAN MELODY   WORDS BY JOHN NEWTON

1. A - maz - ing __ grace how sweet the sound That
2. 'Twas grace that __ taught my heart to fear, And

saved a __ wretch like me! __ I once __ was __
grace my __ fears re - lieved; __ How pre - cious __

lost, but now __ am __ found, Was blind, but __
did that grace __ ap - pear The hour I __

now I see. __
first be - lieved! __

3. Through many dangers, toils, and snares,
   I have already come;
   'Tis grace has brought me safe thus far,
   And grace will lead me home.

4. The Lord has promised good to me,
   His word my hope secures;
   He will my shield and portion be
   As long as life endures.

Sing this vocal countermelody with the melody of "Amazing Grace."

Play a drone on the bells or on the Autoharp throughout the song.

Which instrumental countermelody will you play—the one that uses mostly low tones, or the one that uses mostly high tones?

COUNTERMELODY 1

COUNTERMELODY 2

SECTION 3:
HARMONY AND TEXTURE

INTRODUCTION TO HARMONY AND TEXTURE

Music has melody and harmony. They can be put together in a variety
of ways. The way they are used, separately or together, is called
texture. In this section you will learn more about musical texture.

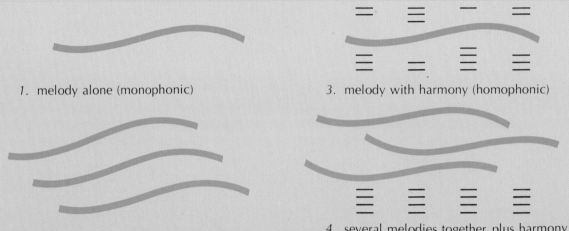

1. melody alone (monophonic)

3. melody with harmony (homophonic)

2. several melodies together (polyphonic)

4. several melodies together plus harmony
   (mixed texture)

Fabrics have texture. The kind of material used, the colors, the
thickness and thinness of yarn, the amount of space between the
strands, the repetitions and contrasts, all add up to something we can
almost feel, even if we do not touch it.

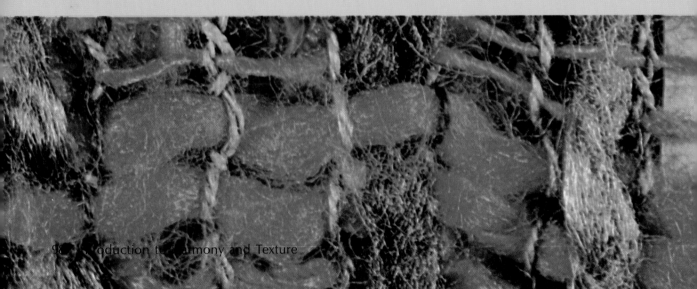

We don't usually feel paintings with our fingers. Yet our eyes tell us that they have a "feel." This visual feel—texture—is an important part of the experience we get from many paintings.

Many things we see give us a sense of texture—of a "feel" they have—whether we touch them or not. Our eyes tell us what our hands would feel if we touched them.

In music, there is nothing for our hands to feel—only sounds. Our ears hear how the sounds go together in melodies and harmonies. We can't see it. We can't touch it. But somehow we can feel it.

Introduction to Harmony and Texture 99

USING WHAT YOU KNOW ABOUT HARMONY AND TEXTURE

Two Different Textures

A melody can be sung alone, creating a texture called *monophonic*.

LET US REJOICE

MUSIC BY CHRISTOPH PRAETORIUS   ENGLISH WORDS BY RICHARD MORRIS

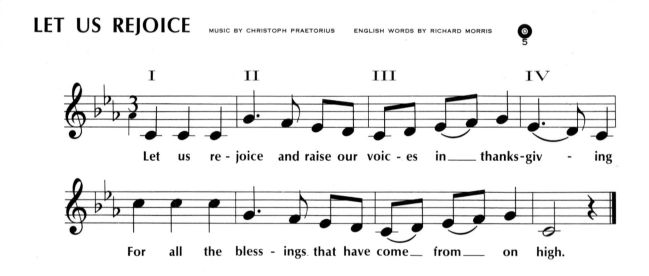

A melody can be played alone, creating a texture called *monophonic*.

PURPLE BAMBOO

FOLK MELODY FROM CHINA

You can change the texture of "Let Us Rejoice" from monophonic to polyphonic by singing it as a two-part round.

After you know the melody of "Hallelujah," sing it as a three-part round. The texture will be polyphonic.

HALLELUJAH

FOLK ROUND FROM ISRAEL

Hal - le - lu - jah,___ hal - le - lu - jah,___ hal - le - lu - jah, hal -

le - lu - jah. Hal - le - lu - jah, hal - le - lu -

jah.___ Hal - le - lu, hal - le - lu, hal - le - lu - jah.___

Melody with Chord Accompaniment

A melody can be accompanied with chords, creating a texture called *homophonic*.

SINNER MAN

BLACK SPIRITUAL

FROM *FOLK SONGSTER* BY LEON AND LYNN DALLIN © 1967 WILLIAM C. BROWN CO., PUBLISHERS USED BY PERMISSION

1. Oh, sin-ner man, where you gon-na run to? Oh, sin-ner man, where you gon-na run to? Oh, sin-ner man, where you gon-na run to, All on that day?

2. **Run to the rock, the rock was a-melting, (*3 times*)**
   All on that day.

3. Run to the trees, trees were a-swaying, (*3 times*)

4. Fall to the earth, earth was a-rolling, (*3 times*)

5. Run to the sea, the sea was a-raging, (*3 times*)

6. Oh, sinner man, you should-a been a-praying, (*3 times*)

7. Oh, sinner man, where you gonna run to? (*3 times*)

"The Drunken Sailor" can be sung as a melody alone (monophonic) and as a melody with chords (homophonic).

THE DRUNKEN SAILOR   CAPSTAN SHANTEY

1. What shall we do   with a drunk - en   sail - or?   What shall we do   with a
2. Hoist him___ up   with a run - ning   bow - line,   Hoist him___ up   with a
3. Put him in the long - boat un - til   he's   so - ber,   Put him in the long-boat un -

drunk - en   sail - or?   What shall we do   with a drunk - en   sail - or
run - ning   bow - line,   Hoist him___ up   with a run - ning   bow - line,
til   he's   so - ber,   Put him in the long - boat un - til   he's   so - ber,

REFRAIN
Ear-lye in the morn-ing? Way, hey, and up she ris-es, Way, hey, and up she ris-es, Way, hey, and

up   she   ris - es   Ear - lye   in   the   morn -   ing.

4. Pull out the plug and wet him all over, . . .   5. Tie him to the mast until he's sober, . . .

6. That's what we do with a drunken sailor, . . .

Discovering the Texture

Before listening to the recording of "The Side Show," look at the score. Can you discover what texture you will hear? Which of the diagrams on page 98 in your book shows the texture?

THE SIDE SHOW WORDS AND MUSIC BY CHARLES IVES COPYRIGHT 1954 BY PEER INTERNATIONAL CORPORATION USED BY PERMISSION.

SING

MUSIC BY VACLAV NELHYBEL   WORDS BY D. DINAND

I sing when I'm hap-py, I sing when I'm glad.
We sing when we're hap-py, we sing when we're glad.

I sing when I feel like cry-ing, I sing when I am
We sing when we feel like cry-ing, we sing when we are

sad. Glad or sad or mad or snap-py,
sad.

sad or glad or mad or hap-py. My cat
You, too,

meows when hap-py, my dog barks when glad. My dad,
when you're hap-py, you, too, when you're sad, should sing

1.
mad or

moth-er, broth-er, sis-ter sing when they are mad or sad or glad or hap-py.
when you feel like cry-ing

2.
way

and you'll feel right a-way all pep-py glad and hap-py yes, yes.

106 Using . . . Harmony and Texture

Hap - py   and glad. _____   Sing!

CALL CHART 7: Texture 🎧
5

Bernstein: *Mass,* "Alleluia"

1 Polyphonic (melody in voices and instruments,
percussion accompaniment)

2 Polyphonic

3 Homophonic (voices singing in chords)

4 Polyphonic

CALL CHART 8: Texture 🎧
5

Handel: *Messiah,* "Hallelujah!" Chorus

   1 Homophonic (melody played by strings)

   2 Mixed (voice melody and orchestra melody with chords)

   3 Monophonic and homophonic alternately

   4 Polyphonic (several melodies in voices and orchestra)

   5 Homophonic (voices and orchestra have melody together)

   6 Monophonic then polyphonic (several melody lines in
voices)

   7 Polyphonic (two melodies overlapping)

   8 Polyphonic (several melodies overlapping)

   9 Polyphonic (two melodies overlapping)

10 Mixed (several melodies plus chords)

11 Homophonic

Four Different Textures

What music texture does each photograph on pages 108 and 109 remind you of?

Listen to four different performances of "Ahrirang." The list below will help you name each texture as you hear it.

1. A melody alone

2. A melody with chords (drone)

3. A melody as a round

4. A melody with countermelody plus chords (drone)

When you know the song, practice one of the instrumental parts on page 110.

You can perform "Ahrirang" in any one of the textures. Which texture will you use in your performance?

AHRIRANG

FOLK SONG FROM KOREA   ENGLISH WORDS BY ALICE FIRGAU

1. Ah - ri-rang, Ah - ri-rang, Ah - ra - ri - yo,_____
2. Ah - ri-rang, Ah - ri-rang, Ah - ra - ri - yo,_____

O - ver the___ hills_____ of___ Ah - ri - rang.
O - ver the___ hills_____ of___ Ah - ri - rang.

Voic - es call me from far_____ a - way._____
Years have passed___ since I went___ a - way._____

I_____ must___ fol - low,___ I___ can - not stay.
Back_____ to___ Ah - ri - rang I'll go_____ some day.

Using . . . Harmony and Texture 109

Plan your own performance of "Ahrirang," using one or more of the parts below.

Recorder (Play throughout)

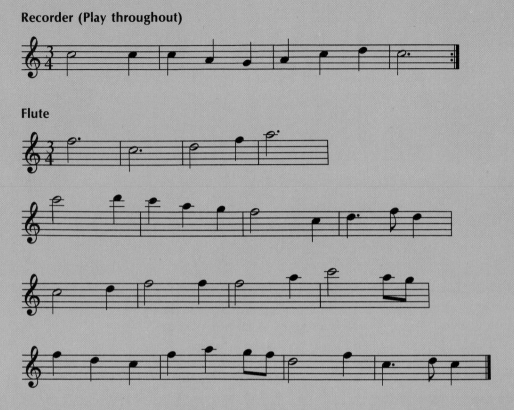

Flute

For an Autoharp accompaniment, pluck an F and a C string together. Use one of these rhythm patterns and play it all through the song.

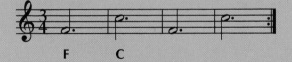

For a bell accompaniment, play the tones F and C, one after the other all through the song. The notation will show you when to play F and when to play C.

F   C

For a bell (or other mallet instrument) accompaniment, play this part.

WHAT DO YOU HEAR? 6: Texture 🔘

What can *you* hear in music? Use these questions as a guide as you listen to one of the pieces listed below. You can listen alone or with a group. You may have to listen several times to answer the questions.

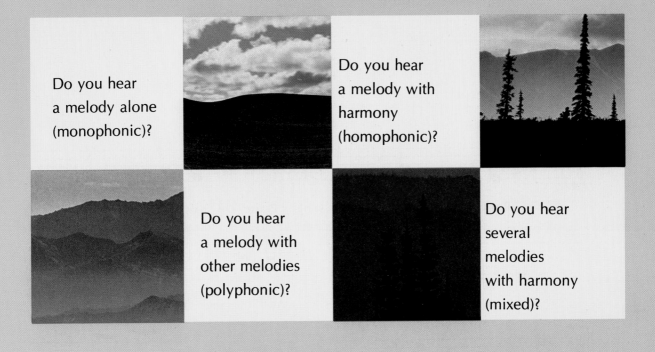

Do you hear a melody alone (monophonic)?

Do you hear a melody with harmony (homophonic)?

Do you hear a melody with other melodies (polyphonic)?

Do you hear several melodies with harmony (mixed)?

1 *Purple Bamboo*

2 Bach: *Trio Sonata No. 1*

3 Bach: *Chorale*

4 Guthrie: *This Land Is Your Land*

5 Verdi: *Aida*, "Grand March"

6 *Gregorian Chant*

When you sing songs for special occasions or in assemblies, be aware of the musical qualities in the music you perform.

Listen to the recording of "Rock of Ages." Do you hear brass, woodwind, or string instruments?

Do the instruments play a melody alone, or a melody with chords? What is the texture?

ROCK OF AGES

TRADITIONAL HEBREW MELODY   ENGLISH WORDS BY G. GOTTHEIL

Rock of A-ges, let our song Praise Thy sav-ing pow - er;

Thou, a-midst the rag'-ing foes, Wast our shel-t'ring tow - er.

Fu-rious they as-sailed us, But Thine arm a-vailed_____ us,

Fu-rious they as-sailed us, But Thine arm a-vailed_____ us,

And Thy word broke their sword When our own strength failed__us.

And Thy word broke their sword When our own strength failed__us.

BATTLE HYMN OF THE REPUBLIC

MUSIC BY WILLIAM STEFFE WORDS BY JULIA WARD HOWE

For percussion parts, see pp. 230 and 231.

1. Mine eyes have seen the glory of the coming of the Lord;
   He is trampling out the vintage where the grapes of wrath are stored;
   He hath loosed the fateful lightning of His terrible swift sword;
   His truth is marching on.

2. He has sounded forth the trumpet that shall never call retreat;
   He is sifting out the hearts of men before the judgment seat.
   Oh, be swift, my soul, to answer Him! Be jubilant, my feet!
   Our God is marching on.

The more parts you add to the texture, the thicker its density. In
which section of this song, A or B, is the density thicker?

SO MY SHEEP MAY SAFELY GRAZE

WORDS AND MUSIC BY ROD McKUEN

ALLELUIA, AMEN

TRADITIONAL ROUND

STYLE: NEW MUSIC

Electronic Sounds

In every period of history some composers have looked for new ways to create music. And as these new ways are created, they are added on to the music that has gone before.

In our times an important thing has happened—the invention of new ways to create sounds by electronic machines. These machines allow composers to do things never before possible with sounds. They can now create extremes of sound that traditional instruments cannot produce.

Here are some of the musical elements that can be extended, or expanded, by using electronic instruments.

1. high . . . low
2. loud . . . soft
3. steps . . . leaps
4. long . . . short
5. thick . . . thin

In some electronic pieces, the sounds are both produced by the instrument (called a *sound synthesizer*) and changed by the instrument according to the composer's wishes.

In this piece, all the sounds except that of the drum were made by electronic instruments. How would you describe what you hear? Is the piece musically "far-out," or experimental? Or does it sound like music you're used to hearing?

6
Resnick: *Yummy, Yummy, Yummy*

In this next piece, all the sounds except the voice were made by electronic instruments. Even the voice sounds were changed electronically. Does this piece sound traditional?

◉ Pousseur: *Trois Visages de Liege,* Movement 1
6

Doris Hays

The next three pieces are different because the original sound for each one was *not* produced by an electronic instrument. In each piece a very common sound was recorded, and then changed by an electronic machine. Can you guess what the original sound was for each piece?

◉ Le Caine: *Dripsody*
◉ Mimargolu: *Bowery Bum*
◉ Bogusky-Reimer: *Dawn Figures*
6

You can record sounds and then change them in many ways by using a tape recorder. The material on pages 118 and 119 will tell you how to do it.

Using a Tape Recorder to Change Sounds

JOYCE BOGUSKY-REIMER

If you have a tape recorder, you can change sounds in several ways. These sounds can then be used to make a musical composition.

On this recording you will hear how some "everyday" sounds have been altered using the speed change dial on a tape recorder. Can you name the original sources?

⊚ *Everyday Sound Collage*
6

Speed changes

Many tape recorders have two speeds. You can change sounds by recording at one speed and playing back at the other.

When you record at high speed and play back at low speed, pitched sounds are one octave lower, the speed is twice as slow, and the quality of the sound changes.

When you record at low speed and play back at high speed, pitched sounds are one octave higher, the speed is twice as fast, and the quality of the sound changes.

⊚ *Speed Changes*
6

Sound with sound

If you have a stereo recorder with two *Record* switches, you can record sound with sound.

Record a sound on *Channel 1*. Rewind the tape and record a second sound on *Channel 2*. Be sure the Record switch for *Channel 1* is off.

CHANNEL 1	SOUND
CHANNEL 2	SOUND

You can also plan to record on *Channel 2* during silent spaces you have left on *Channel 1*. Plan the duration of sound on both channels. Here is an example.

Seconds 0	10″	20″	30″	40″
CHANNEL 1	SOUND		SOUND	
CHANNEL 2		SOUND		SOUND

Follow one of these plans, or think of something else to do. When you play these back, you hear separate sounds from each speaker.

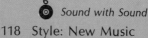
6
⊚ *Sound with Sound*

Sound on sound

When the sounds from two sources are combined on one channel and can no longer be separated, the result is sound on sound. You hear both parts on both speakers.

One way to do this is to play back both channels on which you have recorded sound with sound and record the result on a second tape recorder.

Another way to get sound on sound is to by-pass the erase head (the head closest to the feed reel) when you are recording the second sound.

Either way, record the second sound at a lower volume.

Sound on Sound
6

Making a tape loop

First, record a sound that lasts for 3 or 4 seconds. Make a mark with a white grease pencil or crayon at the beginning and at the end of the sound.

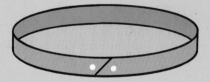

Using a splicing bar, cut out the piece of tape and splice the ends together with splicing tape, forming a loop. Do it carefully so there will be no click or other noise at the point of the splice. Play the loop on a tape recorder and listen to the repeated sound. It can be used as an ostinato in a piece.   Making a Tape Loop
6

Use some of these ideas to create a tape piece of your own. Organize your ideas—put them into a form, use repetition and contrast, vary the dynamics, try to get rhythmic interest, use high and low sounds—try to use some of the things you know about music to make your piece make sense. Here is an example.

Piece for Tape Recorder
6

MORE ABOUT HARMONY AND TEXTURE

Lines of Sound

When you can sing the melody of "Hava nashira," the tones of each phrase create a single horizontal line of sound.

When the tones of all three phrases are sounded together, vertical lines of sounds are created.

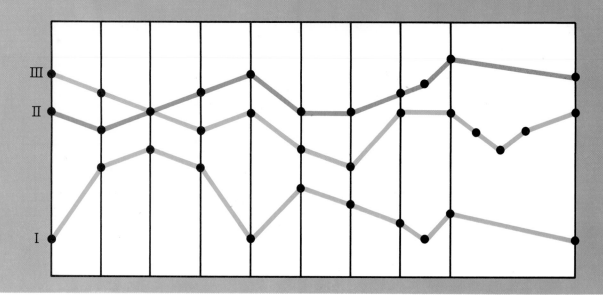

HAVA NASHIRA   ROUND FROM ISRAEL

I
Ha - va na - shi - ra, Shir al - le - lu - ia!

II
Ha - va na - shi - ra, Shir al - le - lu - ia!

III
Ha - va na - shi - ra, Shir al - le - lu - ia!

Changing the Texture

When this melody is performed alone, the texture is monophonic. Play it on flute, recorder, or bells.

CHORALE MELODY
MELODY BY JOHANN SCHOP

For a recorder ensemble, see p. 213.

You can change the texture to homophonic by playing your part along with this recording.

Chorale Melody, Version 1

Listen to another arrangement of the chorale melody. In this version you will hear a mixed texture.

Chorale Melody, Version 2

Now, play your part with Version 2 of the chorale melody.

African Rhythm Complex

Chant each line of the following set of numbers. Clap on the large-size numbers only as you chant.

1. **1** 2 **3** 4 **5** 6 7 **8** 9 **10** 11 **12**

2. **1** 2 3 **4** 5 6 **7** 8 9 **10** 11 12

3. **1** 2 **3 4 5 6 7 8 9 10 11 12**

4. **1 2 3 4** 5 6 **7 8 9 10** 11 12

5. 1 2 **3 4** 5 **6 7** 8 **9 10** 11 12

6. **1 2 3 4 5 6 7 8 9 10 11 12**

Look at the notation for the rhythms you clapped. Choose one of the parts to practice. When the rhythms are added, one at a time, you will hear that each one contributes to the texture of the music.

African Rhythm Complex

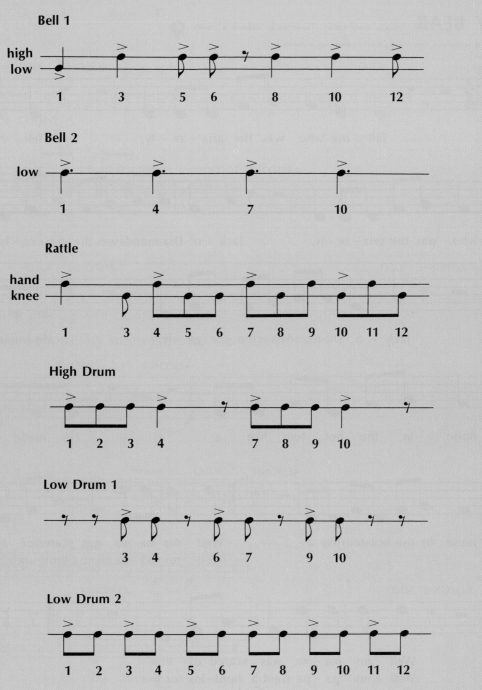

This song, in boogie-woogie style, was written especially for you. Listen for the two sections, A and B.

BOOGIE-WOOGIE

WORDS AND MUSIC BY CARMINO RAVOSA

© 1979 CARMINO RAVOSA

(BASS 1)
Boo - gie - woo - gie,   Boo - gie - woo - gie,

(BASS 2)   (BASS 1)
Boo - gie - woo - gie,   Boo - gie - woo - gie,

(BASS 3)   (BASS 1)
Boo - gie - woo - gie,   Boo - gie - woo - gie.

1. There's a kid that plays pi - an - o on the cor - ner of the street,___ He's
2. Now, this kid that plays pi - an - o on the cor - ner of the street, If you
3. Well, this kid that plays pi - an - o on the cor - ner of the street,___ He's

nev - er had a les - son, but he's got the boo - gie beat. When the
ev - er hear him play___ then you're gon - na have a treat. Now, you
got a wick - ed left___ hand that no - bod - y can beat. He can

kid git a - go - in' you can hear the peo - ple say, "you
peo - ple can look close___ and you peo - ple can look far, But there's
keep that bass a - go - in' and___ nev - er ev - er quit. When it

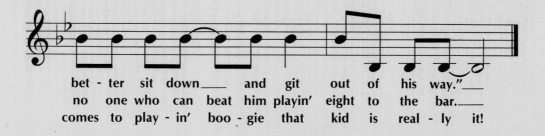

bet - ter sit down____ and git out of his way."____
no one who can beat him playin' eight to the bar.____
comes to play - in' boo - gie that kid is real - ly it!

Here are three walking bass parts you can play on the piano to
accompany section A of the song. The directions in the music
will tell you when to play each one.

Walking bass 1

Walking bass 2

Walking bass 3

Here is another way to play the walking bass parts on the
piano.

Walking bass 1

Walking bass 2

Walking bass 3

More About Harmony and Texture 131

WHAT DO YOU HEAR? 7: Texture 🔘

Listen to the recording. Each time a number is called, choose the word that describes the texture.

Calliet: *Variations on the Theme "Pop! Goes the Weasel"*

---

1 HOMOPHONIC
POLYPHONIC

9 MONOPHONIC
MIXED

---

2 MONOPHONIC
POLYPHONIC

10 MONOPHONIC
HOMOPHONIC

---

3 MONOPHONIC
POLYPHONIC

11 HOMOPHONIC
POLYPHONIC

---

4 HOMOPHONIC
POLYPHONIC

12 HOMOPHONIC
POLYPHONIC

---

5 MONOPHONIC
HOMOPHONIC

13 MONOPHONIC
HOMOPHONIC

---

6 MONOPHONIC
MIXED

14 MONOPHONIC
MIXED

---

7 MONOPHONIC
HOMOPHONIC

15 MONOPHONIC
HOMOPHONIC

---

8 HOMOPHONIC
POLYPHONIC

16 HOMOPHONIC
POLYPHONIC

WHAT DO YOU HEAR? 8: Texture, Tonality 🎧

Listen to the recording. Each time a number is called, choose
the word that describes the texture. Also, decide whether the
music is major, or minor.   Bizet: *L'Arlesienne Suite No. 2,* "Farandole"

1 MONOPHONIC   HOMOPHONIC   POLYPHONIC   MIXED
MAJOR   MINOR

2 MONOPHONIC   HOMOPHONIC   POLYPHONIC   MIXED
MAJOR   MINOR

3 MONOPHONIC   HOMOPHONIC   POLYPHONIC   MIXED
MAJOR   MINOR

4 MONOPHONIC   HOMOPHONIC   POLYPHONIC   MIXED
MAJOR   MINOR

5 HOMOPHONIC
MINOR

6 MONOPHONIC
MINOR

7 MONOPHONIC   HOMOPHONIC   POLYPHONIC   MIXED
MAJOR   MINOR

8 MONOPHONIC   HOMOPHONIC   POLYPHONIC   MIXED
MAJOR   MINOR

9 MONOPHONIC   HOMOPHONIC   POLYPHONIC   MIXED
MAJOR   MINOR

EXPERIENCING THE ARTS: REPRESENTATIONAL, NONREPRESENTATIONAL

When we can easily recognize something in a work of art that represents the world we live in—a person, a house, a flower, an idea—it is said to be *representational*.

What do you think *nonrepresentational* means?

Look at two paintings—the one below, and the one at the top of page 135. Which do you think is representational? Nonrepresentational?

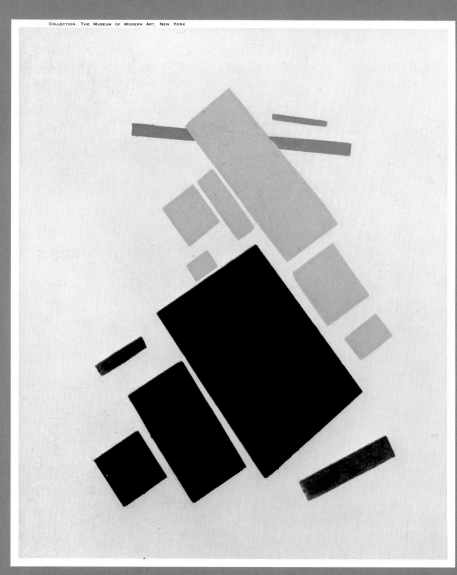

Each kind of art does the same thing—it presents an experience for us to see and feel.

There is representation or nonrepresentation in other arts.

Find an example of each in sculpture and dance on the following two pages.

Music can sometimes suggest a thing or a story. Such music is called *program music*. Much music suggests nothing at all except the sounds themselves. Such music is called *absolute music*.

Listen to these three pieces of music. Two are program music. One is absolute music. Can you tell which is which?

- Copland: *The Red Pony,* "Circus Music"
- Brahms: *Clarinet Sonata,* No. 2
- Mussorgsky: *Pictures at an Exhibition,* "Ballet of Unhatched Chicks"

7

Each work of art is an opportunity for a new experience, whether it represents something we can recognize or is nonrepresentational.

In all works of art, whether we recognize things or not, we *still* perceive and feel.

SECTION 4: FORM

INTRODUCTION TO FORM

In this section you will explore several important forms. You will learn how parts of music are put together in ways that repeat and contrast. When you hear musical parts adding up to whole pieces, you become involved in the experience of musical forming.

The way a building is formed, or organized, is a large part of our enjoyment in seeing it.

The famous Taj Mahal in India uses the form ABA over and over. How many ABA arrangements can you find in the building and the grounds?

Can you find repetition and contrast in the painting at the bottom of pages 138 and 139?

USING WHAT YOU KNOW ABOUT FORM

Two Sections, A and B

As you listen to the recording of this song, notice that it has two sections—A and B. Join in on section B when you can.

FREEDOM from "Shenandoah"

MUSIC BY GARY GELD WORDS BY PETER UDELL

1. Free-dom ain't a state like Maine or Vir-gin-ia,
2. Free-dom ain't a boat that's leav-in' with-out ya,
3. Free-dom is a no-tion sweep-in' the na-tion,

Free-dom ain't a-cross some coun-ty line.
Free-dom ain't a place ya float to find.
Free-dom is the right of all man-kind.

Free-dom is a flame that burns with-in ya,
Free-dom is the how ya think a-bout ya,
Free-dom is a bod-y's 'mag-i-na-tion,

Free-dom's in the state of mind. Free-dom,

free-dom, Free-dom, free-dom.

Free-dom is a flame that
Free-dom is the how ya

burns with-in   ya
think   a - bout   ya,   Free-dom's in the state_____   of   mind.

3.

Free-dom is   a   no - tion sweep-in'   the   na - tion, Free-dom is   a   bod - y's

'mag - i - na - tion, Free-dom is   a   full   time   oc - cu - pa - tion,

Free-dom's in   the   state_____   of   mind!

Soprano recorder

B

1.

2.

Two Sections, A and B

I'M GONNA SING OUT

WORDS AND MUSIC BY DAVID EDDLEMAN

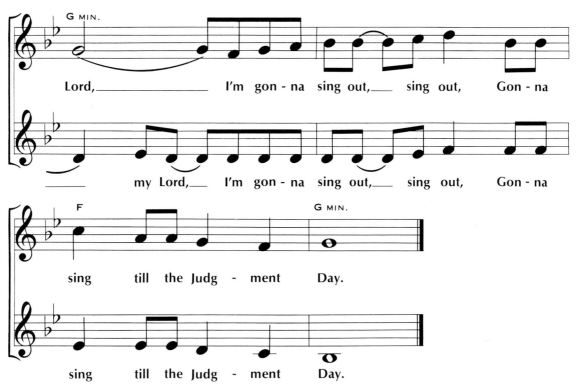

G MIN.

Lord,_____ I'm gon - na sing out,___ sing out, Gon - na

_____ my Lord,___ I'm gon - na sing out,___ sing out, Gon - na

F   G MIN.

sing   till   the   Judg - ment   Day.

sing   till   the   Judg - ment   Day.

For a percussion ensemble, see p. 235.

How will you make section B a contrast of section A? Here are some suggestions.

RHYTHM: contrast of tempo between sections; contrast of rhythm patterns (played on a percussion instrument to accompany the song)

TEXTURE: contrast of melody with harmony to melody alone

DYNAMICS: contrast of loud and soft; getting louder, getting softer

TONE COLOR: contrast in sound of instruments; contrast in use of voices or instruments

Think of other ways to add contrast to your performance.

AB Form

This song has two sections. When you can, sing section B to discover what makes it a contrast to section A.

BABY DAY WORDS AND MUSIC BY MELANIE SAFKA

1. Why sleep when the day has been called out by the sun? From the
2. "Quite, quite," said___ I, "that's all ver - y well to say, But I
3. And I sing it like I heard it; why I heard it, who knows why? Why___

night, 'Cause the light's gon - na shine on ev - 'ry - one. Why
rose be-fore the dawn to your sing - ing yes - ter - day. I
sleep, when___ you can___ watch the sun a - rise? We were

sleep when the sleep on - ly clos - es up our eyes? Why
could - n't see the rising 'cause the dark was in the sky; I
meant to___ see the be - gin - ning of the day. I be -

sleep when we can watch the sun a - rise?
could - n't see the sun 'cause the sun was in my eye."
lieve___ it was planned to lift us this___ way.

Take you an ap - ple and take___ you a song, And watch the ba - by

day __ be __ born; Take you an ap - ple and take __ you a song, And

watch the ba - by day __ be __ born.

CALL CHART 9: Form 🎵

Can you hear sections that repeat and sections that contrast in this piece? Follow the chart to discover the form.

Mexican Cactus

1 INTRODUCTION	7 REPETITION OF A
2 A	8 REPETITION OF A
3 REPETITION OF A	9 CONTRAST B
4 CONTRAST B	10 REPETITION OF A
5 REPETITION OF A	11 CODA
6 INTERLUDE	

ABA Form

Listen to the recording of "Open the Window, Noah" to discover the form. Sing along when you can.

OPEN THE WINDOW, NOAH

BLACK SPIRITUAL

FROM AMERICAN NEGRO SONGS AND SPIRITUALS BY JOHN W. WORK. © 1940, 1968 BY CROWN PUBLISHERS, INC. USED BY PERMISSION OF CROWN PUBLISHERS, INC.

ABC Form

This song has three sections—A, B, and C. Listen to the recording to discover how one section is different from the others.

HAHVAH NAHGEELAH

JEWISH FOLK SONG

EXPERIENCING THE ARTS: Creating Tension

Our lives are full of tension. We often wish there was less of it. But tension, or stress, adds excitement to our lives.

Artists use tension in their works to excite us, to challenge us, to involve our feelings in a new experience. A work of art with no tension in it might be pretty or pleasant, but we wouldn't feel very strongly about it.

In the visual arts (painting, sculpture, architecture, crafts), tension can be caused by these and other qualities.

1. clashes of color
2. irregular lines
3. many different directions
4. things jumbled together

5. contrasting textures
6. distorted shapes
7. off-balance shapes
8. unexpected use of materials

What causes tension in the visual art examples on pages 148–150?

LYONEL FEININGER, VILLAGE STREET. COLLECTION OF THE ART INSTITUTE OF CHICAGO.

Poetry uses tension also. Good poems involve us because they force us to think and feel deeply.

Choose words to finish this familiar little poem. First use words that are very predictable—what everyone would expect. Then choose words that are *unexpected, different, thoughtful, challenging*.

Roses are _____
Violets are _____
Flowers are _____
And so are _____

What qualities seem to cause tension in this poem?

AFRICAN DANCE

The low beating of the tom-toms,
   The slow beating of the tom-toms,
   Low . . . slow
   Slow . . . low—
Stirs in your blood.

             Dance!

A night-veiled girl
   Whirls softly into a
   Circle of light.
Whirls softly . . . slowly,
Like a whisp of smoke around the fire—
   And the tom-toms beat,
   And the tom-toms beat,
And the low beating of the tom-toms
   Stirs your blood.

Langston Hughes

In music, tension and release of tension are created by

1. dynamics
2. tempo
3. density
4. accents

5. tone color
6. rhythm patterns
7. register
8. direction

Experience how these and other qualities are used to create tension and release in the music listed on page 152.

CALL CHART 10: Creating Tension. ◑

Beethoven: *Symphony No. 3, Movement 3*

---

1   First theme; fast; thin to thick density;
     short, even pattern pushes on and on; ◀ and ▶

---

2   Suddenly loud; strong, irregular accents; syncopation;
     sudden louds and softs; fast ♪♪♪ pattern drives on; ◀ builds up;
     contrasting tone colors

---

3   First contrasting theme; change of tone color (French horns);
     ♪♪♪ pattern still heard; ◀ and ▶

---

4   Second contrasting theme; smooth lines going upward
     and downward

---

5   First contrasting theme again; movement slows, then goes on

---

6   First theme again; steady ♪♪♪ pattern, driving on and on;
     contrasting registers; contrasting tone colors; ◀ builds up

---

7   Loud first theme; strong, irregular accents; syncopation;
     loud and soft; ♪♪♪ pattern continues; ◀ builds up

---

8   Coda (ending section); soft, then driving to a loud,
     strong final cadence

STYLE: Improvisation

Improvising—creating music "on the spot"—has been used throughout the history of music. Sometimes, composers give an outline of a melody and its harmony and expect the performer to fill in the outline by improvising.

Improvisation is widely used today, especially in jazz. Listen to this recording of a 12-bar blues improvisation. What instrument plays the melody? What instrument plays the accompaniment?

⊙
8 *12-Bar Blues Improvisation*

In *Some of These Days* you will hear how a singer uses her voice to improvise on a melody. Also, you will hear how a group of instumentalists (string bass, piano, percussion) improvise an accompaniment.

⊙
8 Brooks: *Some of These Days*

What instrument improvises on a melody you may know on this recording?

⊙
8 *When the Saints Go Marching In*

Now listen to some music that was written by a composer who lived long ago. First you will hear the composer's outline. Then you will hear the performer's improvisation.

⊙
8 Corelli: *Sonata for Violin and Harpsichord,* No. 3, "Adagio"

Another kind of improvisation is used in *chance music.* In some chance music a composer gives general directions, but always gives the performer freedom to choose—to improvise.

For example, the performer may choose from several different tempos or dynamics. In other chance music a composer creates most of the piece, but at certain points asks the performer to improvise random sounds.

Listen to this recording. Two performers are heard improvising at the same time (two tapes combined). One performer improvises on the keyboard of an organ; the other improvises sounds from inside the organ.

⊙
8 Wolff: *For 1, 2, or 3 People*

WHAT PEOPLE DO WITH MUSIC; THE CONDUCTOR

Some music is performed by one person (solo), by two (duet), by three (trio), by four (quartet), by five (quintet). When a piece calls for a larger group of performers, such as a chorus, a band or an orchestra, a leader is needed—a person who keeps everyone together and who makes the musical decisions. This musical leader is called a *conductor*.

A conductor has many special skills and many responsibilities. Listen to Lena McLin, a famous choral conductor, discuss her work.

◉ *Interview with Lena McLin*
◉ *The Rehearsal*
◉ *The Performance*

The conductor and performers prepare for the performance during rehearsal. In the next recording, you will hear Lena McLin at rehearsal—teaching, demonstrating, drilling—getting all the details worked out so the music can come through as it should.

And now the performance. The preparation is over and the final result is shared with the audience.

MORE ABOUT FORM

Phrases—Repetition, Contrast

In the piece *Dueling Banjos,* a guitar and a banjo have a
musical duel. Do the phrases use mostly repetition, or contrast?

Listen for some other qualities that are used throughout the piece.

1. low and high registers
2. tempo changes
3. tones that move mostly by step
4. upward and downward direction

🎯 Scruggs: *Dueling Banjos*

In conversation, it is natural to *respond* to a question. Some
music uses the question-and-answer, or call-and-response, idea.
In songs, the call is often sung by a solo voice and the response
by a group—the chorus.

TONGO FOLK SONG FROM POLYNESIA SET DOWN BY GLADYS RUSTAY, OBERLIN 🎯

FROM TAYOYUMAWIT, COURTESY OF WORLD AROUND SONGS, BURNSVILLE, N.C.

Listen to the recording of "Woke Up This Morning." What can you discover about the phrases?

WOKE UP THIS MORNING

FREEDOM SONG   ADAPTED WITH NEW LYRICS BY ROBERT ZELLNER

© COPYRIGHT 1963, 1966 BY FALL RIVER MUSIC INC.   ALL RIGHTS RESERVED   USED BY PERMISSION

1. I woke up this morn - ing with my mind_____ stayed_____ on free - dom,__ I woke up this morn - ing with my mind_____ stayed_____ on free - dom,__ I woke up this morn - ing with my mind_____ stayed_____ on free - dom,__ Hal - le - lu,_____ _____ Hal - le - lu, hal - le - lu,__ hal - le - lu - - jah!__

2. Walk-in' and talk - in' with my mind_____ stayed_____ on free - dom,__ Walk-in' and talk - in' with my mind_____ stayed_____ on free - dom,__ Walk-in' and talk - in' with my mind_____ stayed_____ on free - dom,__ Hal - le - lu,_____

3. **Singin' and prayin' with my mind stayed on freedom, (3 times)**
   Hallelu, hallelu, hallelujah!

4. **Body in prison but my mind stayed on freedom, (3 times)**
   Hallelu, hallelu, hallelujah!

Listen for the call and response parts in this music.

Call and Response Collage

12-Bar Blues Form

"Till That Day Blues" is an example of the 12-bar blues form. Look at the score to discover some things about this form.

How many phrases are there?

Which phrases have the same words?

Do any of the phrases have the same melody contour?

Play the recording of "Till That Day Blues" and notice that the piano fills in the breaks in the melody at the end of each phrase.

📖 For a percussion ensemble, see p. 233.

TILL THAT DAY BLUES
WORDS AND MUSIC BY SOL BERKOWITZ

© 1973 SOL BERKOWITZ

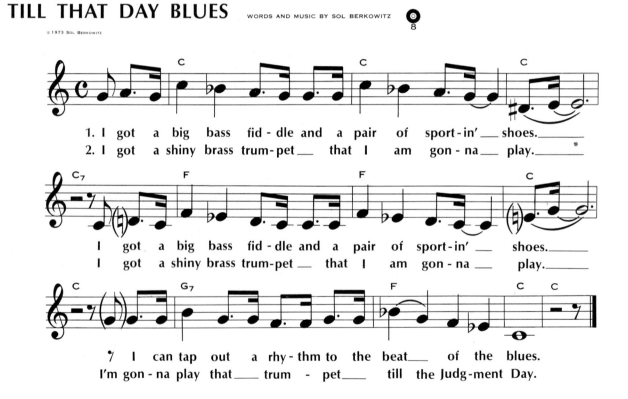

1. I got a big bass fid-dle and a pair of sport-in' __ shoes. __
2. I got a shiny brass trum-pet __ that I am gon-na __ play. __

I got a big bass fid-dle and a pair of sport-in' __ shoes. __
I got a shiny brass trum-pet __ that I am gon-na __ play. __

I can tap out a rhy-thm to the beat __ of the blues.
I'm gon-na play that __ trum - pet __ till the Judg-ment Day.

Now, make up your own response and fill in the break in the melody at the end of each phrase. You can improvise a voice part to sing on the syllable "doo," or you can make up a rhythm pattern to play on a percussion instrument.

Practice the Autoharp chords for "Till That Day Blues." They follow a form called the 12-bar blues, a form that was developed in the United States many years ago.

Each of the three phrases in the blues form has a special pattern of chords. This diagram shows how the three phrases, with their chords, are used to form a 12-bar blues song. The dotted lines show where the breaks occur in the melody.

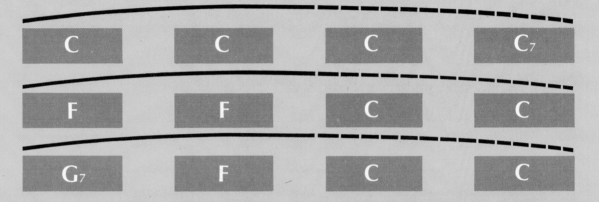

If a stereo record player is available, accompany the melody track of "Till That Day Blues" by playing the chords on the Autoharp. Try strumming this pattern all through the song. Notice the accents.

T means thumb; F means finger.

Now listen to two pieces that are based on the 12-bar blues form. The first one is a classical blues piece; the other is a "rock" blues piece that is played on an electronic sound instrument.

Armstrong: *Gut Bucket Blues*
8

Porcupine Rock
9

Rondo Form

You have heard and performed music with one contrasting section. Now listen for two contrasting sections in this piece.

The chart will help you discover how the sections are put together to create a rondo form.

CALL CHART 11: Rondo Form 🔊

Rameau: *Gigue en rondeau*

---

1 FIRST SECTION A
Melody in high register; repeated tones in low
    register; meter

---

2 CONTRASTING SECTION B
Two melodies together; moves mostly by step;
polyphonic texture

---

3 REPEAT OF A

---

4 ANOTHER CONTRASTING SECTION C
Starts as a canon (like a round); polyphonic texture

---

5 REPEAT OF A

RAGTIME

Ragtime, a style of music developed in the United States, has repeated sections as well as several contrasting sections. Each section is the same length and uses many syncopated rhythms.

The chart will help you hear the structure of the music and some of its other qualities.

CALL CHART 12: Ragtime 🎧
Joplin: *Fig Leaf Rag*

---

1 INTRODUCTION

---

2 SECTION A: Repeated rhythm pattern; steady beat in lower register; melody mostly outlines chords

---

3 SECTION B: Different rhythm pattern; steady beat continues; melody moves mostly by step; harmony in thirds

---

4 SECTION A: Repetition of number 2

---

5 SECTION C: Another rhythm pattern; thicker density; steady beat continues; melody in upward and downward direction

---

6 SECTION D: Melody has many repeated tones; still another syncopated rhythm pattern; melody is ornamented; steady beat continues in lower register; thicker density continues to syncopated ending

---

Canon Form

In a canon, each voice or instrument performs the same melody, but each starts at a different time.

When "Alas, Alack" is performed as a canon, the texture is polyphonic.

What is the texture when "Alas, Alack" is performed as a melody alone?

ALAS, ALACK   MUSIC BY TERENCE GREAVES   WORDS BY WALTER DE LA MARE

FROM FOLLOW MY LEADER BY TERENCE GREAVES. USED BY PERMISSION OF OXFORD UNIVERSITY PRESS. LONDON.

Ann, Ann, come quick as you can! There's a fish that talks in the

fry - ing pan. Out of the fat, as clear as glass, He

put up his mouth__ and moaned, "A - las," Oh, most mourn-ful "A -

las, a - lack!" Then turned to his siz - zling and sank him back.

Now listen to a canon played on two recorders.

Telemann: *Six Canonic Sonatas*, No. 1, Movement 3

As you listen again, try to hear other things in the music—wide leaps, trills that decorate the melody, long and short sounds, syncopation, notes that are played staccato (separated, detached).

Theme and Variations

When one musical idea is repeated in a different version in each section of a piece, the form is theme and variations. The chart will help you hear how a composer uses musical qualities to vary a theme.

CALL CHART 13: Theme and Variations 🎵

Handel: *The Harmonious Blacksmith*

	THEME:	Slow; major; many strong cadences; melodies move by steps and leaps
1	VARIATION 1:	Many short sounds in higher register; faster tempo; major
2	VARIATION 2:	Same tempo as variation 1; short sounds in lower register; use of ornamentation
3	VARIATION 3:	Short sounds in higher register; long sounds in lower register; faster tempo
4	VARIATION 4:	Short sounds in lower register; long sounds in higher register; same tempo as variation 3
5	VARIATION 5:	Fastest tempo; many short sounds moving stepwise; downward and upward direction; strong cadence at the end

WHAT DO YOU HEAR? 9: Form 🎵

Each time a number is called you will hear two musical examples. Decide whether the second example is a repetition of the first, or whether it is a contrast or a variation.

1	REPETITION	CONTRAST	VARIATION
2	REPETITION	CONTRAST	VARIATION
3	REPETITION	CONTRAST	VARIATION
4	REPETITION	CONTRAST	VARIATION
5	REPETITION	CONTRAST	VARIATION
6	REPETITION	CONTRAST	VARIATION
7	REPETITION	CONTRAST	VARIATION
8	REPETITION	CONTRAST	VARIATION

La Sinda
Roll an' Rock
Brahms: *Waltz, Op. 39, No. 2*
Mozart: *Symphony No. 36, Movement 3*
Beethoven: *Variations on "God Save the King"*
Sakura
Chopin: *Waltz in E Flat, Op. 18*
El Capotin

LIVE! LIVE!

WORDS AND MUSIC BY MARIA JORDAN

La la la la la la la la, la la la la la la la la, La la la la la la la la,

la la la la. Do, do, so much is worth do-ing; Try, try what-
Run, run, there's worlds to dis-cov - er! Fly, fly wher-
See, see what's hap-pen-ing 'round you; Feel, feel the

ev - er your heart would go! Dance, dance, the mu-sic is call - ing,
ev - er you want to try! Dream, dream, and keep on pur - su - ing,
shake of a friend - ly hand. Taste, taste the sweet and the so - ur,

Sing, sing a song that you know.
Reach, reach for stars in the sky! Look at the world a-round you and you'll see that
March, march, and play in a band!

life's an ad-ven-ture in a way. So get up and go and grab a-hold of it! There's

D.S. (last time al ⊕)

liv-ing to do each day,_____ and no rea-son for de - lay. Come on, let's go and

liv - ing, so much liv-ing to do each day!_____ There's

liv-ing to do!

165

There are two sections in this song. Section A starts on low C.
On what note does section B start?

TURN, TURN, TURN (To Everything There Is a Season)

WORDS FROM THE BOOK OF ECCLESIASTES   ADAPTATION AND MUSIC BY PETE SEEGER

To ev-'ry-thing, (Turn, turn, turn) There is a sea-son (Turn, turn, turn) And a time for ev-'ry pur-pose un-der heav-en.

Fine

1. A time to be born, a time to die; A time to plant, a time to reap; A time to kill, a time to heal; A time to laugh, a time to weep.
2. A time to build up, a time to break down; A time to dance, a time to mourn; A time to cast a-way stones, A time to gath-er stones to-geth-er.
3. A time of love, a time of hate; A time of war, a time of peace; A time you may em-brace, A time to re-frain from em-brac-ing.
4. A time to gain, a time to lose; A time to rend, a time to sew; A time to love, a time to hate; A time for

To ev - 'ry peace, I swear it's not too

D.S. al Fine

late._____ To ev - 'ry -

Section B can be sung as a canon with a countermelody.
The countermelody can be sung, or it can be played on
recorder and bells.

(I) II

A time to be born, a time to die; A time to plant, a time to

Countermelody

Turn, Turn, Turn, Turn, Turn,

reap; A time to kill, a time to heal; A time to laugh, a time to weep.

Turn, Turn, Turn, Turn, Turn, Turn Turn.

EXPERIENCING THE ARTS: Multimedia

The words in the spinner below describe several qualities of sound. Experiment with different ways to create these sound qualities. Use voices or instruments.

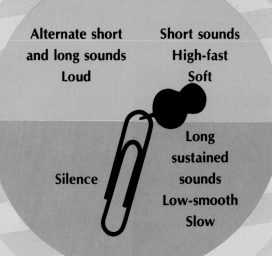

These same words can be used to describe qualities of body movement. They can also be used to describe things you can do with a flashlight—shining it against the ceiling, the walls, or the floor. Experiment with different ways to create movements and light effects, using what the words in the spinner suggest.

Now create a multimedia presentation that combines sounds, movements, and light effects.

1. Make two spinners (like those at the top of page 169) out of heavy cardboard. Use a pushpin to fasten a paper clip in the center of each circle. To spin the paper clip, flick the end with your finger.

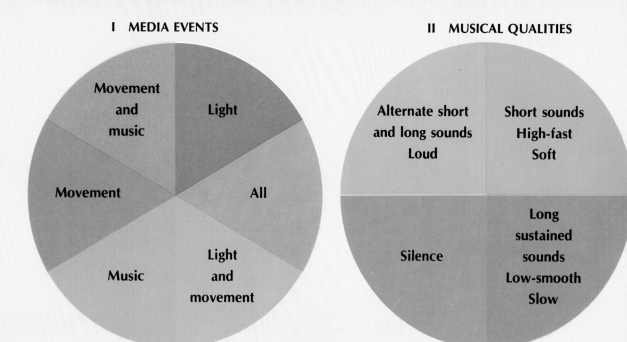

I   MEDIA EVENTS

- Movement and music
- Light
- All
- Light and movement
- Music
- Movement

II   MUSICAL QUALITIES

- Alternate short and long sounds / Loud
- Short sounds / High-fast / Soft
- Long sustained sounds / Low-smooth / Slow
- Silence

2. Divide the performers into four groups.

Group 1: voices
Group 2: instruments
Group 3: dancers
Group 4: flashlights

3. Make a plan for your presentation.

- Spin each wheel and write down what it shows. For example, spinner I—Movement and music; spinner II—Long-sustained

- Decide how many such events you will use.

- Decide how long each event will last.

- Decide and practice what will happen for each event.

Here is an example of a plan.

	0″	30″	40″	50″	60″

I	movement and music	light	light and movement	all
II	long sustained-smooth-low-slow	silence	alternate short and long sounds-loud	short sounds high-fast-soft

4. Present your multimedia performance.

Afterward, take time to judge the results. Did all parts go well together? Did any part call too much attention to itself?

EXPERIENCING THE ARTS

What happens when we experience art?

JULES BRETON, THE SONG OF THE LARK, COLLECTION OF THE ART INSTITUTE OF CHICAGO.

OUR SENSES receive the sounds of music, the colors in a painting, the movement of dancers, the word-images in a poem. Most experiences of art require seeing, or hearing, or both.

OUR MINDS AND FEELINGS GET INVOLVED with all the things happening in the music or painting or sculpture or dance. We notice what is there and respond to the qualities as if they were inside our feelings.

WE CREATE ART by singing, playing, composing, painting, dancing, acting. This gives us another way to experience art. We become creators and experiencers at the same time, and produce something others can experience.

WE ANALYZE AND JUDGE ART when we study how a work of art is made and whether we think it is made well—with skill, with sensitivity, with imagination. We analyze and judge our own creations as well as the work of others.

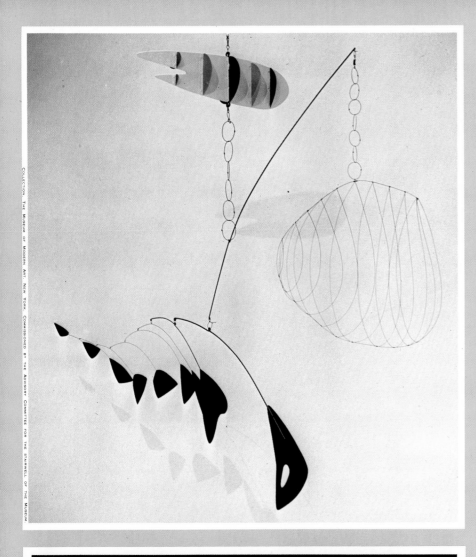

WE VALUE ART if we find excitement in experiencing and creating music, poems, crafts, dances, plays. The arts become part of our lives to enjoy and experience. Just think of how much would be missing from our lives if we didn't have the arts!

171

GEE, IT'S NICE TO BE ALONE

WORDS AND MUSIC BY ROD McKUEN

Relaxed

(Gee, it's nice to be a-lone, To wake up by your-self; To
(Gee, it's nice to be a-lone, To get to know your-self; To

own the day a-while, And not have to talk to an-y-bod-y.
waste a-way the time, And

not have to smile for an-y-bod-y. What a deal to stay in your pa-

ja-mas, ___ With noth-in' ver-y much to do, But watch the shad-ows

chang-ing ___ pan-o-ra-mas, ___ When e-ven the shad-ows ___ don't look

back at you. ___ Well, gee, it's nice to be a-lone, To find out for your-

self, What sol-i-tude's a-bout; And not have a need

for an-y-bod-y. Gee, it's nice to be a-lone. . .some-times. ___

ON MY JOURNEY

BLACK-AMERICAN TRADITIONAL SONG   ARRANGED BY LAWRENCE EISMAN

NEW VERSES BY FRED HELLERMAN, LEE HAYS, RONNIE GILBERT, AND ERIK DARLING

Relaxed

1.
1. When I'm on my jour-ney, oh, don't you weep,___
2. Ev - 'ry riv - er must go home to the sea,___
3. On the moun - tain leave my sor - rows be - low,___

MELODY

2.
1. When I'm on my jour-ney,___ don't you weep af - ter me,___
2. Ev - 'ry lone - ly riv - er___ must go home to the sea,___
3. High up on the moun-tain___ leave my sorrows down be-low,___

1.
When I'm on my jour - ney, oh, don't you weep,___
Ev - 'ry riv - er must go home to the sea,___
On the moun - tain leave my sor - rows be - low,___

2.
When I'm on my jour - ney,___ don't you weep af - ter me,___
Ev - 'ry lone - ly riv - er___ must go home to the sea,___
High up on the moun-tain___ leave my sorrows down be - low,___

1.
When I'm on my jour - ney, oh, don't you weep,___
Ev - 'ry riv - er must go home to the sea,___ I don't
On the moun - tain leave my sor - rows be - low,___

2.
When I'm on my jour - ney,___ don't you weep af - ter me,___
Ev - 'ry lone - ly riv - er___ must go home to the sea,___ I don't
High up on the moun-tain___ leave my sorrows down be - low,___

1.
want you to weep af - ter me._____

2.
want you to weep af - ter me._____

174   Singing in Chorus

WATERS RIPPLE AND FLOW

FOLK SONG FROM CZECHOSLOVAKIA   ENGLISH WORDS BY MARGARET FISHBACK

Smoothly

1. Wa - ters rip - ple and flow,____ Swift - ly flow____ to the sea,
2. Riv - er Tu - ra flow - ing, Hear my yearn - ing____ song.

Bring my free - dom to me, Set my spir - it____ free.
For my home____ I long, Ev - er make__ me__ strong.

Riv - er flow - ing by On your way__ to the sky.
Tu - ra flow - ing deep, Let me cour - age__ keep.

3. Sound the cry____ of free - dom, Riv - er, as __ you __ flow,

Then my heart__ might know Vic - t'ry o - ver__ woe.

Tu - ra, flow - ing past, Give me lib - er - ty at last.

THREE WHITE GULLS

FOLK SONG FROM ITALY   ARRANGED BY DAVID S. WALKER

ENGLISH WORDS BY MARGUERITE WILKINSON

ORIGINAL TITLE "THE THREE DOVES" BY MARGUERITE WILKINSON FROM BOTSFORD COLLECTION OF FOLK SONGS—VOLUME 3. COPYRIGHT © 1921, 1922 G. SCHIRMER, INC. USED BY PERMISSION.

1. There are three_____ white gulls_____ a - fly - ing;_____ There are
2. In the waves_____ they dip_____ their soft wings;_____ In the

three_____ white gulls_____ a - fly - ing;_____ There are three_____ white gulls a-
waves_____ they dip_____ their soft_____ wings;_____ In the waves_____ they dip their

fly - ing;_____ By the sea they cry, By the sea they cry, By the sea they
soft wings;_____ Then__ soar to the sky, Then__ soar to the sky, Then__ soar to the

cry.
sky.   Ti-ra - li - ra - lu, Ti-ra-li - ra - lu, Ti-ra-li - ra - lu._____

GREEN, GREEN

WORDS AND MUSIC BY BARRY MCGUIRE AND RANDY SPARKS   ARRANGED BY MILTON FRIEDMAN

With a Steady Beat
INTRODUCTION*

REFRAIN

mf Doot - doo, doo, doo, doo, doo__ wah!   Green, green, it's green, they say,__ on the

mf Doot - doo, doo, doo, doo, doo__ wah!   Green, green, it's green, they say,__ on the

mf Doot - doo, doo, doo, doo, doo__ wah!   Green, green, its green, they say,__ on the

far side of the hill;___ oo_____   Green, green, I'm go - in' a - way__ to where the

far side of the hill;___ oo_____   Green, green, I'm go - in' a - way__ to where the

far side of the hill;___ oo   Green, green, I'm go - in' a - way__ to where the

*Voice 1 enters first; add voice 2; add voice 3.

grass is green-er still.__ Ah_____

grass is green-er still.__ Ah_____

1. Well I told my ma-ma on the day I was born,__ "Don-cha
grass is green-er still.__ 2. No there ain't no-bod-y in this whole__ wide world__ gon-na
3. I don't care__ when the sun__ goes down,__ Where I

1. cry when you see I'm gone._____
2. tell me how to spend my time._____ Ah_____
3. lay my__ wear-y head._____

1. cry when you see I'm gone.__
2. tell me how to spend my time.__ Ah_____
3. lay my__ wear-y head.__

cry when you see I'm gone.__ You know there ain't no-bo-dy gon-na
tell me how to spend my time.__ I'm__ just a good__ hap-py
lay my__ wear-y head.__ Green, green val-ley or a

got - ta be a - trav - el - in' on.____
bud - dy could you spare me a dime?____   A - sing-in'
there I'm gon - na make__ my bed.____   (*Repeat to Fine.*)

got - ta be a - trav - el - in' on.____
bud - dy could you spare me a dime?____   A - sing-in'
there I'm gon - na make__ my bed.____   (*Repeat to Fine.*)

set - tle me down,__ I just   got - ta be a - trav - el - in' on."____
ram - bl - in' man,____ say   bud - dy could you spare me a dime?____   A - sing - in'
rock - y road,____ It's   there I'm gon - na make__ my bed.____   (*Repeat to Fine.*)

THOU, O LORD, ART MY SHEPHERD

MUSIC BY BENEDETTO MARCELLO   WORDS BY R. J. S. STEVENS

Thou, O Lord,_____ art____ my Shep - herd,

Thou, O Lord,_____ art____ my Shep - herd,

There - fore shall_____ I____ want noth - ing, There - fore shall

There - fore shall_____ I____ want noth - ing, There - fore shall

I want noth - ing, There - fore shall I_____ want

I want noth - ing, There - fore shall I_____ want

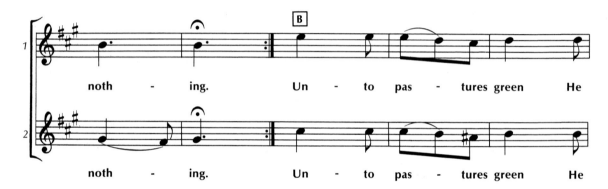

noth - ing. Un - to pas - tures green He

noth - ing. Un - to pas - tures green He

lead - eth me; He lead - eth me be - side_____ the

lead - eth me; He lead - eth me be - side_____ the

wa - ters of com - fort. No e - vil

wa - ters of com - fort.

BIDIN' MY TIME

MUSIC BY GEORGE GERSHWIN   ARRANGED BY SOL BERKOWITZ   WORDS BY IRA GERSHWIN

I'm bid - in' my time;_____ 'cause that's the kind - a guy I'm._____ While oth - er folks grow diz - zy I keep bus - y Bid - in' my time. Next year,___ next year,___ some - thin's bound to hap - pen;___ This year,___ this year,___ I'll just keep on nap - pin',___ And bid - in'___ my

time _____ 'cause that's the kind-a guy I'm._____ There's

no re-gret-tin' When I'm set-tin' bid-in' my

time. There's bid-in' my time._____

SING A RAINBOW

WORDS AND MUSIC BY ARTHUR HAMILTON   ARRANGED BY MARILYN COPELAND DAVIDSON

COPYRIGHT © 1955 BY MARK VII MUSIC, INC., LOS ANGELES, CALIFORNIA. USED BY PERMISSION.

Moderately Ⓐ
mp

Red and yel-low and pink and green, pur-ple and or-ange and

mp
Red and yel-low and___ pur-ple, or-ange,

mp
Red and yel-low, pink, green, pur-ple, or-ange,

CODA

rit. D.S. al ⊕ *f* *rit.*

1
me._____ Sing a rain-bow, Sing a rain-bow, too._____

2
3
me. (with me.__) Sing a rain-bow, Sing a rain-bow, too._____

I DON'T MIND WORDS AND MUSIC BY DAVID EDDLEMAN

With a good swing

A F Bb F C7
I don't mind__ if you sing;__ I don't mind__ if you dance;__
La la la__ la la la,__ La la la__ la la la,__

F Bb
I don't mind__ as long as you don't mind__ if
La la la__ la la la la la la__ la

|1.,2. *No repeat first time* |3.
F C7 C7 F
I should sing,__ too, just by chance.__ *(Section B)*
La la la__ la la la la.__ la la la.__

B F Bb F C7
f You'll nev-er go wrong keep-ing a song sing-ing a-long. You'll
la la la la la la la la la la la la la, La

F Bb F
see you've got to be hap-py and free sing-ing a
la la la la la la la la la la la la

|1.,2. |3.
C7 C7 F
mel-o-dy. La
la la la. La la la la.__

LIFE HAS LOVELINESS

MUSIC BY ROBERT J. POWELL   WORDS BY SARA TEASDALE

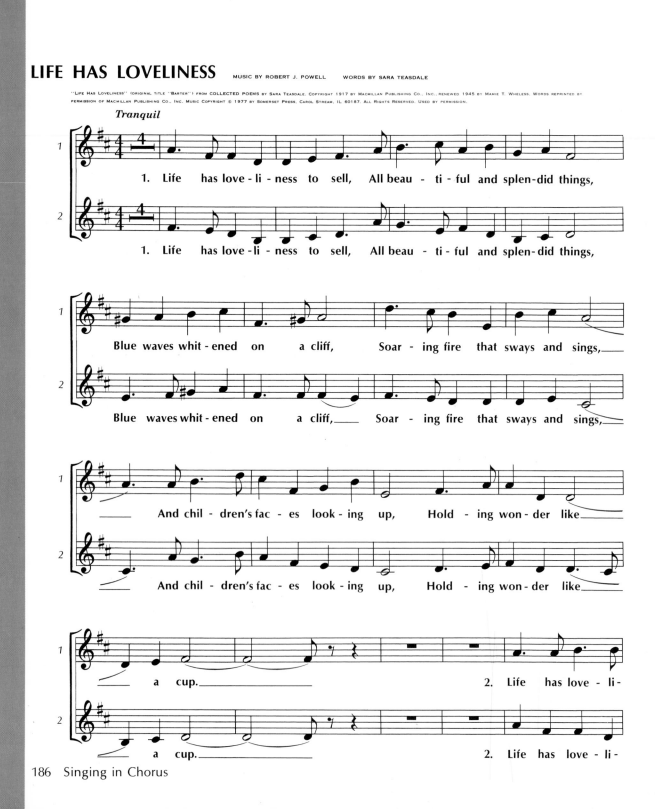

1. Life has love-li-ness to sell, All beau-ti-ful and splen-did things,

Blue waves whit-ened on a cliff, Soar-ing fire that sways and sings,____

____ And chil-dren's fac-es look-ing up, Hold-ing won-der like____

a cup.____   2. Life has love-li-

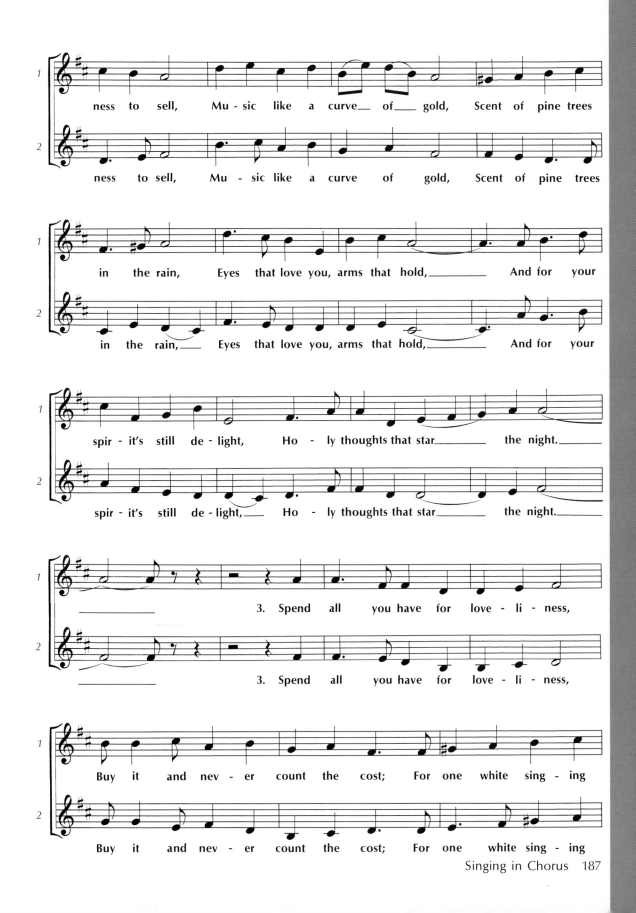

hour of peace Count man-y a year of strife well lost,_____ And for a

hour of peace Count man-y a year of strife well lost,_____ And for a

breath of ec-sta-sy Give all you have been or could_____ be._____

breath of ec-sta-sy Give all you have been or could_____ be._____

GLORY TO GOD   MUSIC BY LUDWIG GEBHARDI   WORDS TRADITIONAL

I Glo - ry to God in the high - est!

II Peace on the earth, on the earth_____ peace And good-

III will to men, to_____ all_____ men. A -

IV - - - men, A - men.

PLAYING THE GUITAR

◉

If you have never played guitar, begin by studying "Playing the Guitar," *Silver Burdett Music, Book 5.*

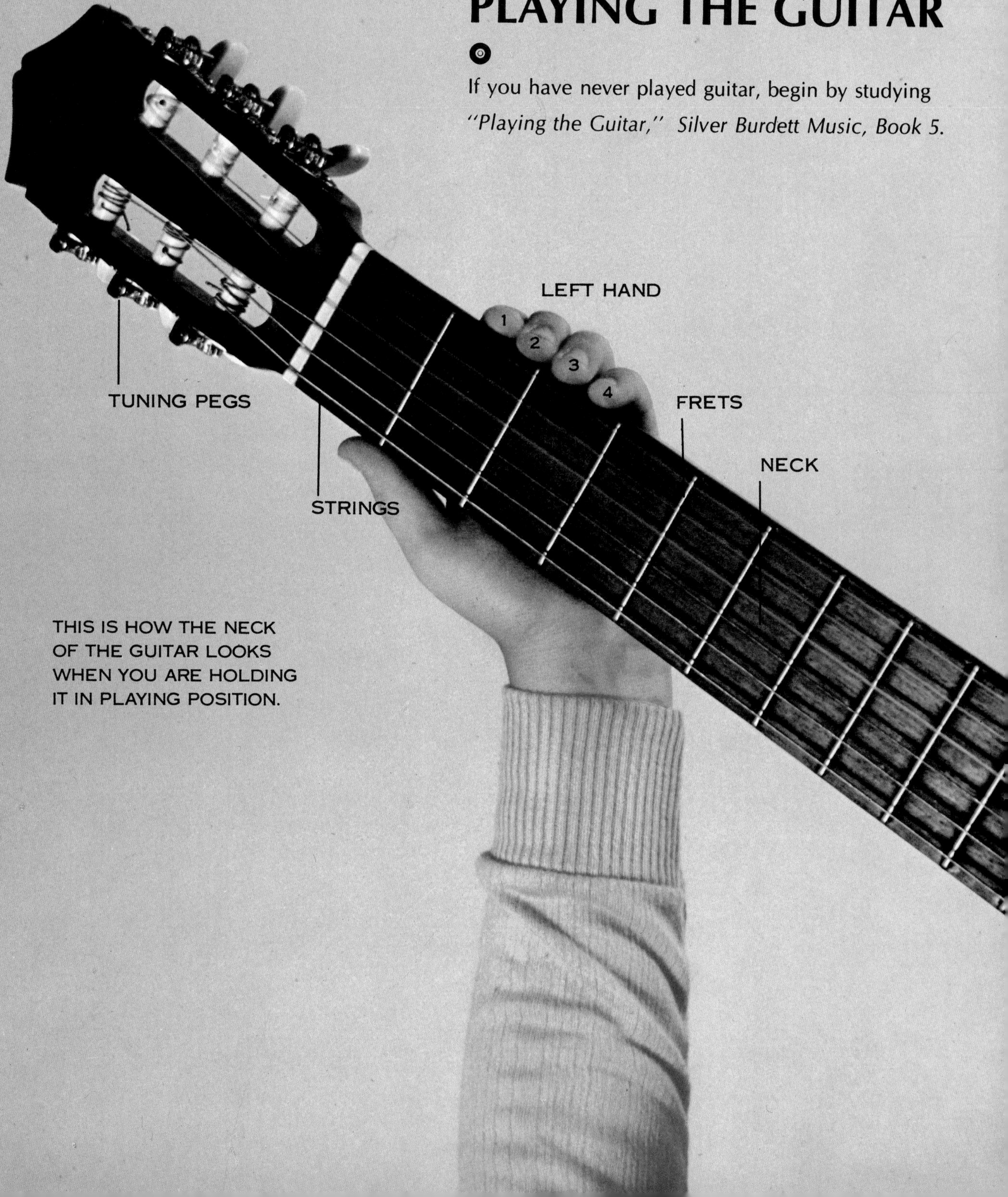

LEFT HAND

1
2
3
4

TUNING PEGS

FRETS

NECK

STRINGS

THIS IS HOW THE NECK
OF THE GUITAR LOOKS
WHEN YOU ARE HOLDING
IT IN PLAYING POSITION.

These diagrams will show you a simplified way to play the C and G_7 chords on the guitar.

To play the C chord, put finger 1 (your index finger) on the B string. Strum the strings shown in red.

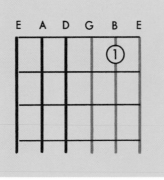

To play the G_7 chord, move finger 1 to the high-E string and strum the strings shown in red.

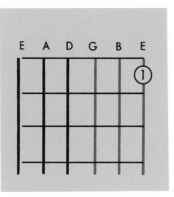

If you have already played the simplified C and G_7 chords, try the full chords.

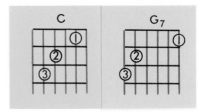

Use the C and G_7 chords to accompany this song.

GOODBY, OLD PAINT

Practice changing back and forth from the C chord to the G_7 chord by accompanying one of the songs you may know.

- "Chumbara," page 33
- "Puttin' On the Style," page 34
- "La Sinda," page 35

If you cannot play the full C and G_7 chords easily, team up with a friend who will play a bass part while you strum the simplified chords.

To play a bass part, alternate these two bass notes when the simplified C chord is played.

Alternate these two bass notes when the simplified G_7 chord is played.

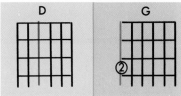

Use the C and G_7 chords to accompany "Mary Ann."

MARY ANN

THE A AND E₇ CHORDS

When you can play the A and E₇ chords, you will be able to accompany more songs. The photographs and diagrams will show you where to place your fingers.

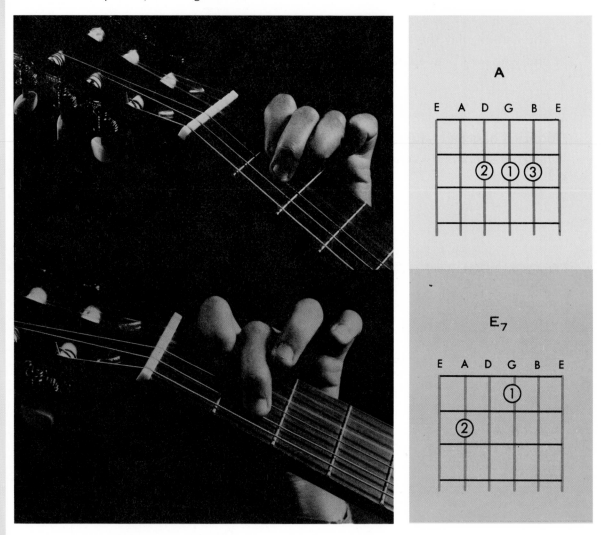

Sing and accompany by ear some two-chord songs you know using the A and E₇ chords.

- "I'se the B'y," page 10
- "La Raspa," page 26
- "There's a Fiesta," page 27
- "Take Time in Life," page 31
- "Gonna Build a Mountain," page 78

The easiest way to strum is to brush your thumb down across the strings in a rhythm that fits the song you are accompanying.

BACK-AND-FORTH STRUM

Brush your thumb across the strings, moving away from your body. This is the *downstroke,* shown by an arrow (↓). Between downstrokes, strum the strings again, moving toward your body. This is the *upstroke,* shown by an arrow (↑).

Begin with a simple pattern of downstrokes and upstrokes in a regular rhythm. Be careful to strum only the strings needed for the chord you are playing.

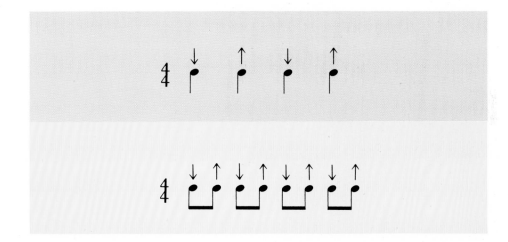

Play the A and E₇ chords to accompany "Ain't Gonna Rain." Follow the arrows above the words and use the back-and-forth strum.

AIN'T GONNA RAIN

        A   E₇

↑ ↓ ↑ ↓ ↑ ↓ ↑ ↓ ↑ ↓ ↑ ↓ ↑ ↓ ↑ ↓
The | woodchuck, he's a ┤ choppin' wood, The | possum, he's a ┤ haulin'.

↑ ↓ ↑ ↓ ↑ ↓ ↑ ↓ ↑ ↓ ↑ ↓ ↑ ↓ ↑ ↓   A

My | poor old dog fell | off a log And | killed himself a ┤ bawlin'.

↑ ↓ ↑ ↓ ↑ ↓ ↑ ↓ ↑ ↓ ↑ ↓ ↑ ↓ ↑ ↓   E₇

It | ain't gonna rain, it | ain't gonna rain, It | ain't gonna rain no | more.

↓ ↑ ↓ ↑ ↓ ↑ ↓ ↑ ↓ ↑ ↓ ↑ ↓ ↑ ↓   A

Come on down, | ev'rybody sing. It | ain't gonna rain no | more.

THE D-MINOR AND A₇ CHORDS

Practice playing two more chords. The photographs and the diagrams will show you where to place your fingers.

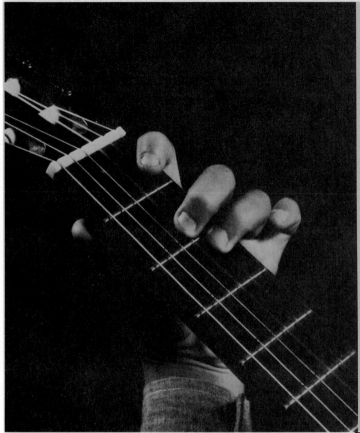

THE D-MINOR CHORD

Here is the fingering for the D-minor chord.

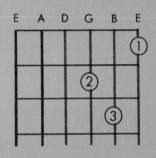

When you accompany "Joshua Fit the Battle of Jericho," use this fingering for the A₇ chord.

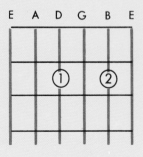

Use the back-and-forth strum to accompany "Joshua Fit the Battle of Jericho." Try one section at a time. Follow the arrows above the words and play the same strumming rhythm throughout.

JOSHUA FIT THE BATTLE OF JERICHO

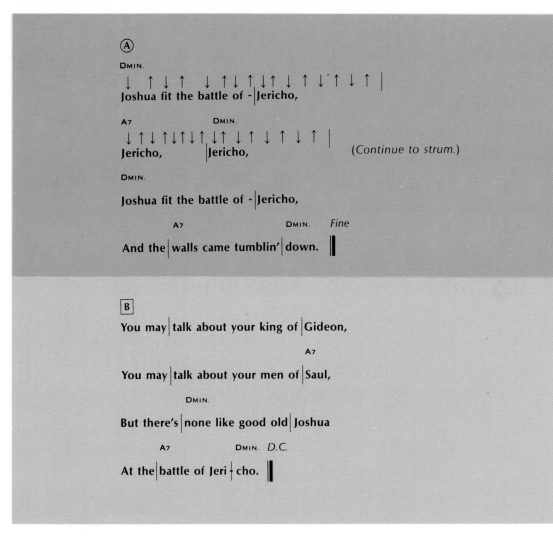

Now, use the D-minor chord with the C chord to accompany these songs.

- "Sinner Man," page 102
- "The Drunken Sailor," page 103

Notice the fingering for the D chord in the diagram below. Compare it with the fingering for the D-minor chord on page 194.

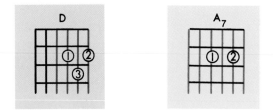

Use the D and A$_7$ chords to accompany "He's Got the Whole World in His Hands." Try one of the strums suggested on page 197.

HE'S GOT THE WHOLE WORLD IN HIS HANDS

    (A7)   D

1. He's got the |whole   world |in His hands, |

                 A7   D

He's got the |whole wide world |in His hands,

He's got the|whole   world |in His hands,

                 A7   D

He's got the |whole world in His |hands.

2. He's got the wind and the rain . . .
3. He's got the little bitty baby . . .
4. He's got you and me brother . . .
5. He's got the whole world . . .

MORE ABOUT STRUMS

Here are some rhythm patterns to use when playing the back-and-forth strum.

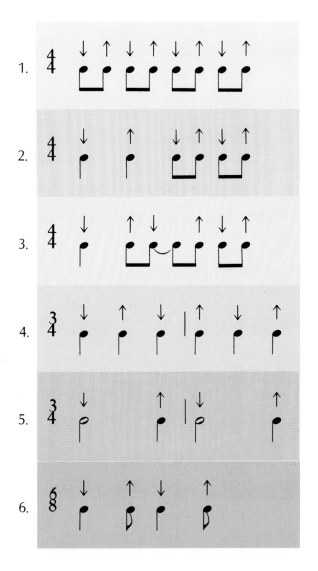

You can create your own rhythm pattern to match the style of the song you are accompanying. Experiment! You might invent a strumming rhythm nobody has ever used before.

To vary the sound of the back-and-forth strum, use the tips of your fingers rather than your thumb. As you strum on the downstroke with your fingers, you will hit the strings with your fingernails, making a sharp sound.

Remember to hold your fingers loosely so they will brush the strings easily. Experiment to find the sound you like.

Practice the D and A_7 chords by accompanying this song. Make up a strum of your own.

OLD BLUE

VERSE

1. I had an old dog,_____ And his name was Blue,_____ _____ And I bet-cha five dol-lars he's a good dog, too. Come on Blue,__ you good dog,_ you;__ Come on Blue,_____ you good dog,_ you._____

2. I grabbed my axe and I tooted my horn,
   Gonna git me a 'possum in the new-ground corn. *Refrain*

3. Chased that ol' 'possum up a 'simmon tree,
   Blue looked at the 'possum, 'possum looked at me. *Refrain*

4. Blue grinned at me, I grinned at him,
   I shook out the 'possum, Blue took him in. *Refrain*

5. Baked that 'possum all good and brown,
   And I laid them sweet potatoes 'round and 'round. *Refrain*

6. Well, old Blue died, and he died so hard,
   That he shook the ground in my back yard. *Refrain*

7. I dug his grave with a silver spade,
   I let him down with a golden chain. *Refrain*

8. When I get to heaven, first thing I'll do,
   Grab me a horn and blow for old Blue. *Refrain*

CHORD FAMILY, KEY OF A (A E_7 D)

Practice these fingerings; then accompany the songs below.

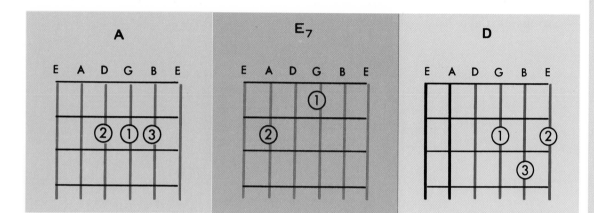

ON TOP OF OLD SMOKY

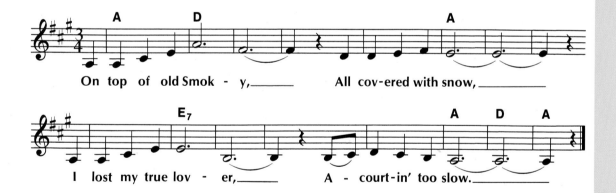

On top of old Smok - y,_____ All cov-ered with snow,_____

I lost my true lov - er,_____ A - court-in' too slow._____

SILENT NIGHT

A E_7 A
Silent night, holy night, All is calm, All is bright

D   A
Round yon Virgin, Mother and Child.

D   A
Holy Infant so tender and mild,

E_7 A E_7 A
Sleep in heavenly peace, Sleep in heavenly peace.

CHORD FAMILY, KEY OF D (D A₇ G)

Practice these fingerings, then accompany "Tzena, tzena" and the songs on page 201.

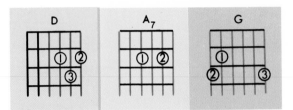

TZENA, TZENA

Tze - na, tze - na, tze - na, tze - na, come in - to the fields and we'll be -
Hoe - ing, sow-ing, new things grow-ing, pi - o - neer-ing all to - geth - er,

gin_____ to work the land.
come _____ and lend a hand.

Tze - na, tze - na, build-ing a new na-tion, toil - ing bus - i - ly all

day._____ Soon we'll dance and have a cel - e - bra-tion, But

first we'll work and then we'll play.

NEW RIVER TRAIN

1. I'm rid-in' on that new ri-ver train. I'm rid-in' on that new ri-ver train. The same old train that brought me here, gon-na car-ry me back a-gain. Oh, dar-lin' you can't love_ one, Oh, dar-lin' you can't love_ one, You can't love one and have a-ny fun, Oh, dar-lin' you can't love one.

JOHN JACOB JINGLEHEIMER SCHMIDT

John Ja-cob Jing-le-heim-er Schmidt, That's my name too. When-ev-er I go out, The peo-ple al-ways shout, "There goes John Ja-cob Jing-le-heim-er Schmidt," Da Da Da Da Da Da Da Da.

CHORD FAMILY, KEY OF G (G D₇ C)

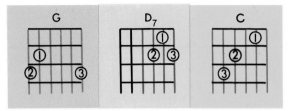

Practice using the G, D₇, and C chords by accompanying songs you know. Some of these songs use two chords (G, D₇), others use three chords (G, D₇, C).

- "I'se the B'y," page 10
- "The John B. Sails," page 14
- "La Raspa," page 26
- "There's a Fiesta," page 27

- "Take Me Home, Country Roads," page 28
- "Take Time in Life," page 31
- "Gonna Build a Mountain," page 78
- "Amazing Grace," page 96

You can accompany "Viva l'Amour" with the G, D₇, and C chords.

VIVA L'AMOUR

Make up your own strumming pattern to accompany the singing of "Rock Island Line." For suggestions, see page 197.

ROCK ISLAND LINE

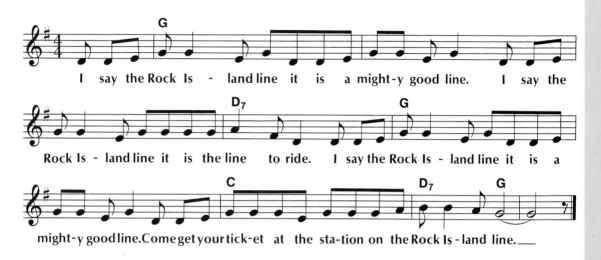

I say the Rock Is - land line it is a might-y good line. I say the Rock Is - land line it is the line to ride. I say the Rock Is - land line it is a might-y good line. Come get your tick-et at the sta-tion on the Rock Is - land line.___

With the chords that you now know, you will be able to accompany two- or three-chord songs in the following keys. (In addition, you may know the E-minor chord from "Playing the Guitar," *Silver Burdett Music 5.*)

KEY OF C	C		G₇
KEY OF D MIN.	D MIN.		A₇
KEY OF D	D	G	A₇
KEY OF G	G	C	D₇
KEY OF A	A	D	E₇

A WORD ABOUT TUNING

Tune the low-E string to a piano or to a pitch pipe. Place your finger just behind the fifth fret as shown in the diagram. You will be fingering the correct pitch for the next string, the A string. As you pluck the fingered string, tune the A string until the pitches match.

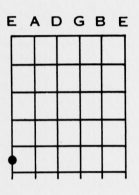

These pairs of strings should sound the same pitch when one of them is fingered as shown.

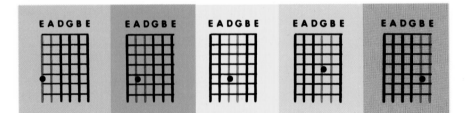

When you first start, it will be easier to have someone tune the guitar for you. Watch carefully and listen to learn how it is done. Then try tuning it by yourself.

Remember, a good guitar player always plays on a well-tuned instrument.

⊙ PLAYING THE RECORDER

This satellite will help you learn to play the soprano and alto recorders. If you need help with the fingerings for the first few pages, study the fingering chart on page 220.

PRIVATE PRACTICE

Review these notes: B A G on the soprano recorder;
E D C on the alto recorder.

SUO GAN

DANCE TUNE

ENSEMBLE

Add these parts while others sing "La Raspa." Ask someone to play an
Autoharp or guitar accompaniment.

LA RASPA   (Song on page 26.)

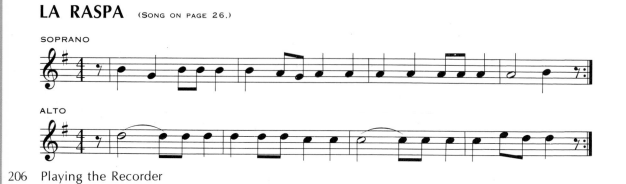

PRIVATE PRACTICE

Review these notes: high C and D on the soprano recorder;

high F and G on the alto recorder.

WINTER, ADE! (Winter, Goodby!)

SOPRANO

Win - ter, a - de! Win - ter, a - de! It may be sad to — part

But laugh - ter fills my — heart, Win - ter, a - de! Win - ter, a - de!

ALTO

ENSEMBLE

The soprano and alto parts for *Winter, Ade!* can be played together.
Ask someone to play an Autoharp accompaniment.

PRIVATE PRACTICE

Review these notes: low E D C on the soprano recorder;

low A G F on the alto recorder.

TIDEO

SOPRANO

ALTO

Review F# on the soprano recorder and B on the alto recorder by practicing the refrain of "Open the Window, Noah." Then practice the other parts on pages 208 and 209.

OPEN THE WINDOW, NOAH (SONG ON PAGE 146)

THE STREETS OF LAREDO

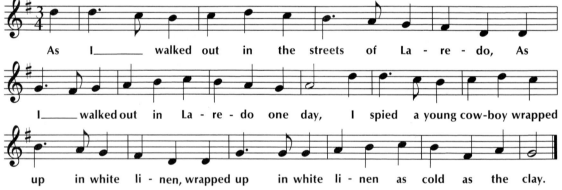

As I_____ walked out in the streets of La - re - do, As I_____ walked out in La - re - do one day, I spied a young cow-boy wrapped up in white li - nen, wrapped up in white li - nen as cold as the clay.

MICHAEL FINNEGAN

ENSEMBLE

Organize an ensemble by "mixing and matching" the melodies and countermelodies on pages 208 and 209.

OPEN THE WINDOW, NOAH (SONG ON PAGE 146)

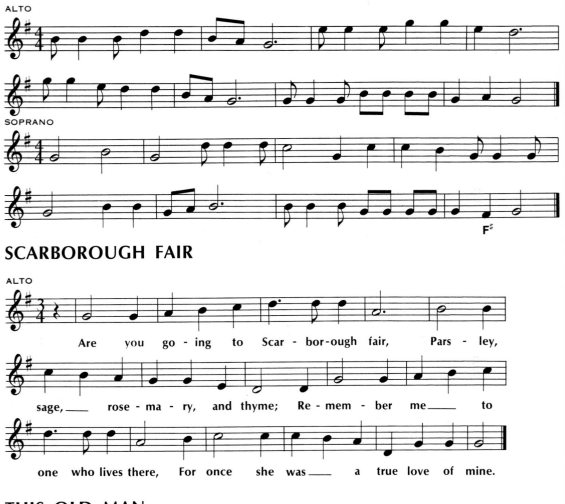

SCARBOROUGH FAIR

Are you go - ing to Scar - bor - ough fair, Pars - ley,

sage, ___ rose - ma - ry, and thyme; Re - mem - ber me ___ to

one who lives there, For once she was ___ a true love of mine.

THIS OLD MAN

ENSEMBLE

This piece uses notes you know. Choose a part to practice. Then team
up with other recorder players to make an ensemble.

BRANSLE DE CHAMPAIGNE BY CLAUDE GERVAISE

"BRANSLE DE CHAMPAIGNE" FROM RENAISSANCE DEBUT ARRANGED BY MAURICE C. WHITNEY. REPRINTED BY PERMISSION OF CONSORT MUSIC., A DIVISION OF MAGNAMUSIC.

A NEW NOTE

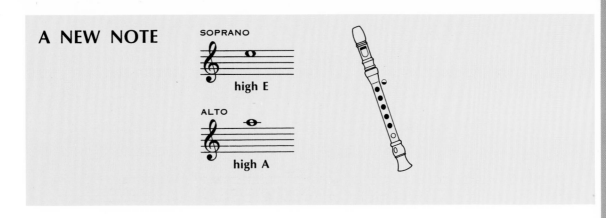

SOPRANO
high E

ALTO
high A

PRIVATE PRACTICE

The soprano recorder can practice the melody of "Lonesome Valley" on page 59.

LONESOME VALLEY

ALTO

A

ENSEMBLE

When the soprano recorder plays the melody of "Lonesome Valley," the alto recorder can add this countermelody.

ALTO

PRIVATE PRACTICE

The soprano recorder can practice the melody of "Purple Bamboo" on page 100.

PURPLE BAMBOO

ENSEMBLE

After you can play these melodies, team up with other recorder players. Then play each melody through at least two times. Parts II, III, and IV follow in turn, two measures apart.

CANON IN C   BY DAVID EDDLEMAN   ©1978 DAVID EDDLEMAN

CANON IN F   BY DAVID EDDLEMAN   ©1978 DAVID EDDLEMAN

ENSEMBLE

Choose a part to practice. Then team up with another recorder player to make an ensemble.

CHORALE MELODY

ANOTHER NEW NOTE

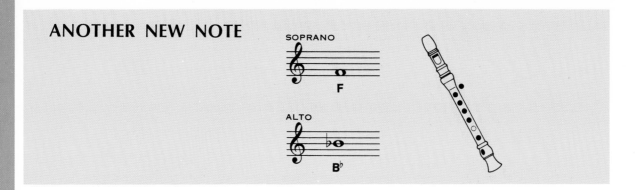

PRIVATE PRACTICE

I'LL BEGIN AHEAD OF YOU

SOPRANO

I   II   III

I'll   be - gin   a - head   of   you,   You'll   be - gin   be - hind   me;
I   will   stay   a - head   of   you,   And   you   will   not   find   me.

ALTO

I   II   III

ENSEMBLE

Team up with other recorder players and play "I'll Begin Ahead of You" as a two- or three-part round. Add these parts to the ensemble.

ALTO (PLAY WITH SOPRANO ABOVE.)   SOPRANO (PLAY WITH ALTO ABOVE.)

TWO NEW NOTES

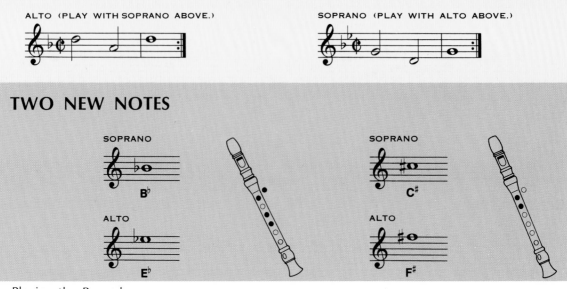

PRIVATE PRACTICE FOR SOPRANO RECORDER

Now that you know the fingerings for B♭ and C♯, you can play the following melodies on the soprano recorder.

The *John B.* Sails, page 14
The Baby Boy, page 50

Carol from an Irish Cabin, page 49
Everybody's Got a Song, page 58

PRIVATE PRACTICE FOR ALTO RECORDER

Now that you know the fingerings for E♭ and F♯, you can play the following melodies on the alto recorder.

My Dame Hath a Lame, Tame Crane (countermelodies), page 30
Take Time in Life (countermelody), page 31
Anthony Mayberry (verse), page 56
Amazing Grace (countermelody 2), page 97

Read about the 12-bar blues on pages 158 and 159 in your book. Then practice this blues song on the soprano or the alto recorder.

CORNBREAD, PEAS, AND BLACK MOLASSES

SOPRANO AND ALTO

1. I don't want no,____ corn - bread, peas, and black mo - las - ses.____
2. I ain't got no,____ got no read - y made___ mon - ey.____

I don't want no,____ corn-bread, peas, and black mo - las - ses.____
I ain't got no,____ got no read - y made___ mon - ey.____

At sup - per time, Lord, at sup - per____ time.____
To call my own, Lord, to call my____ own.____

ENSEMBLE

Ask someone to play the Autoharp chords when you play "Cornbread, Peas, and Black Molasses" on the recorder. Have others sing the song to fill out the ensemble.

DOUBLE ROUND

Add these ostinatos to the ensemble.

Add this part for bells or mallet instruments to the ensemble.

FINAL ENSEMBLES

Play the ensembles on pages 217–219 with friends who play the soprano or the alto recorder.

POLKA

SOP I
SOP II

MELODY
Al-though I do not like to dance, I real-ly must ad-mit when

ALTO

MELODY

SOP I
SOP II

some-one plays a pol - ka tune, I sim-ply can't re-sist. At

ALTO

SOP I
SOP II

an - y time of day or night, If sud-den-ly by chance,

ALTO

SOP I
SOP II

MELODY
That pol - ka sound should fill the air, my feet be-gin to dance.

ALTO

DEEP BLUE SEA

Deep blue sea, ba - by, deep blue sea,

*A[#] FINGERING SAME AS B^b

Deep blue sea, ba - by, deep blue sea,

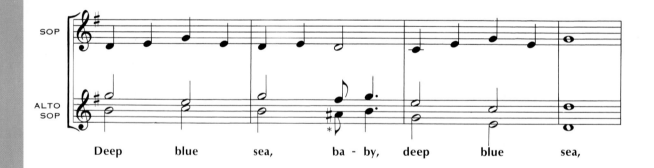

Deep blue sea, ba - by, deep blue sea,

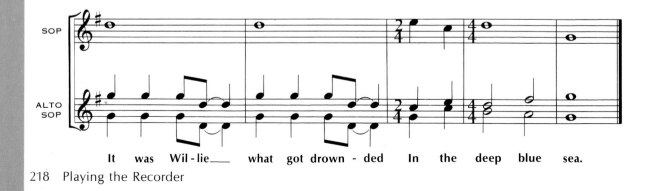

It was Wil - lie____ what got drown - ded In the deep blue sea.

ANGELS WE HAVE HEARD ON HIGH

SOP I

An - gels   we   have heard   on high,   Sweet - ly   sing - ing   o'er   the plains,
And   the moun - tains   in   re - ply,   Ech - o - ing   their joy - ous strains.

SOP II

ALTO

SOP I

Glo — — — — — — — — ri - a

SOP II

ALTO

SOP I

in   ex - cel - sis De - o,   De - o.

SOP II

ALTO

FINGERING CHART

SOPRANO

| C | D | E | F | F# | G | A | Bb | B | C | C# | D | Eb | E |

ALTO

| F | G | A | Bb | B | C | D | Eb | E | F | F# | G | Ab | A |

READING RHYTHM

12

You have already played some percussion parts to accompany songs you know. Sometimes you play alone and sometimes in an ensemble. This satellite contains arrangements for two or more percussion instruments that can be used to accompany songs in your book. Play any one of the parts alone with the recording. Or organize a group of friends to play in an ensemble.

LA RASPA (SONG ON PAGE 26)

To feel the steady beat in "La Raspa," play an Autoharp accompaniment as you sing the song.

This Autoharp part is in $\frac{4}{4}$ meter. The steady beat is shown as a quarter note (♩). The beats are measured in sets of 4—four beats in each measure. Notice that the measures are separated by bar lines.

Press the G or D₇ button as indicated and strum each quarter note.

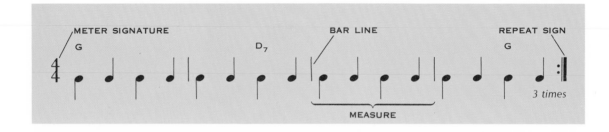

For a special Autoharp strum, play short strokes with your thumb on the lowest strings for the notes with the stems down. For notes with stems up, brush the strings in the opposite direction with your fingers.

Here are two percussion parts to play with "La Raspa." The tambourine part shows the steady beat in quarter notes and quarter rests (𝄽). In the castanets part, some beats are divided into two equal sounds. These sounds are shown as eighth notes (♫).

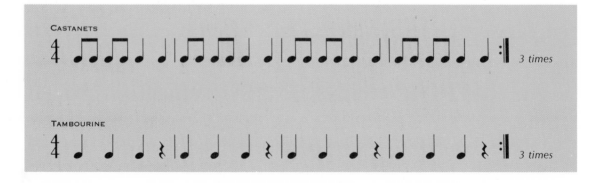

Remember: In $\frac{4}{4}$ meter
• a quarter note (♩) shows a beat of sound;
• a quarter rest (𝄽) shows a beat of silence;
• 2 eighth notes (♫) show the beat divided into two equal sounds.

JOY TO THE WORLD (SONG ON PAGE 4)

Here is an Autoharp part you can play with the refrain of "Joy to the World."

The meter signature ($\frac{4}{4}$) tells you that there are four beats in a measure and that a quarter note gets one beat.

The Autoharp part uses quarter notes (♩) and half notes (♩).

The chord letters will tell you when to play the D, A₇, or G chord.

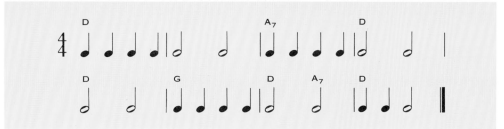

Here are two percussion parts to play with the refrain of "Joy to the World." The tambourine part uses half notes (♩) and half rests (━).
The wood block part uses quarter notes (♩) and quarter rests (𝄾).

Remember: In $\frac{4}{4}$ meter
• a half note (♩) shows two beats of sound;
• a half rest (━) shows two beats of silence.

LA SINDA (SONG ON PAGE 35)

To feel the steady beat in "La Sinda," play a percussion part as you listen to the song.

This percussion part for wood block is in $\frac{3}{4}$  meter. The steady beat is shown as a quarter note. The beats are measured in sets of 3—three beats in each measure.

Start playing on the first strong beat.

WOOD BLOCK

♩ *Play throughout.*

In this percussion part for tambourine, you will play only on the first beat of every measure. Start playing on the first strong beat.

TAMBOURINE

Play throughout.

Team up with a friend and play both percussion parts together.

Now try an Autoharp accompaniment for "La Sinda" that uses dotted half notes (𝅗𝅥.). In $\frac{3}{4}$ meter you will hold a dotted half note for three beats.

Start playing the Autoharp on the first strong beat. The chord letters will tell you when to change from one chord to another.

AUTOHARP

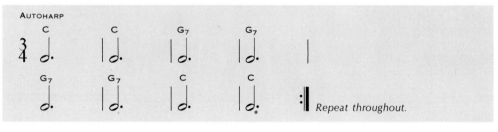

Repeat throughout.

Remember: In $\frac{3}{4}$ meter
• a dotted half note (𝅗𝅥.) is held for three beats.

THERE'S A FIESTA (SONG ON PAGE 27)

To feel the beat moving in sets of 3, play an Autoharp
accompaniment as you listen to "There's a Fiesta." Play short strokes
with your thumb for notes with stems down. For notes with stems
up, brush the strings in the opposite direction with your fingers.

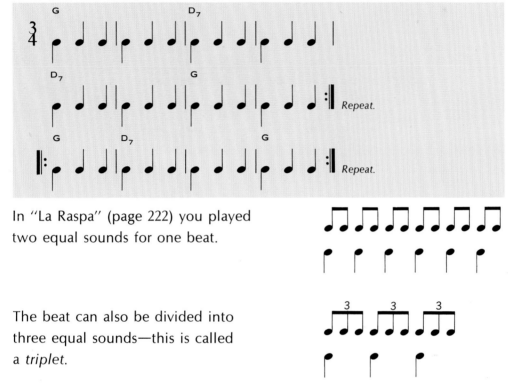

In "La Raspa" (page 222) you played
two equal sounds for one beat.

The beat can also be divided into
three equal sounds—this is called
a *triplet*.

Try one of the parts in this arrangement for tambourine and wood
block as you listen to the recording of "There's a Fiesta."

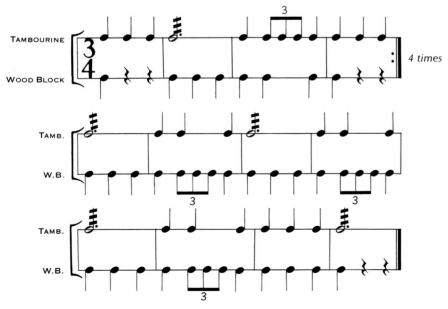

I'SE THE B'Y (SONG ON PAGE 10)

This song is in $\frac{6}{8}$ ($\frac{2}{\text{J.}}$) meter. The steady beat is shown as a dotted quarter note (J.).

To feel the steady beat, play this Autoharp accompaniment as you sing "I'se the B'y."

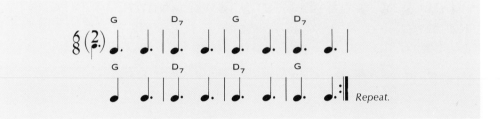

You will find these three different rhythms in the percussion arrangement at the bottom of the page.

Now try playing one of these parts with the recording.

GONNA BUILD A MOUNTAIN (SONG ON PAGE 78)

The meter signature $\math{C}\!\!\!\!|$ tells you that there are two beats in a measure and that a half note ($\downarrow$) gets one beat. Which part shows the steady beat in the percussion arrangement below?

Choose one of the parts to practice.

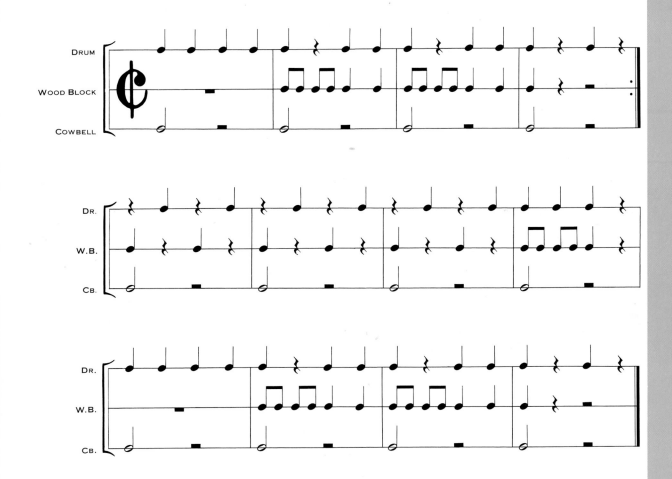

After you have practiced your part, add it to the other two parts and form an ensemble to accompany the singing. Before you play, decide how fast or how slow you will play.

ORION (SONG ON PAGE 70)

Practice one of the parts to accompany "Orion." Notice that the meter changes from $\frac{4}{4}$ to $\frac{3}{4}$ in the middle of the music. The quarter note will get one beat throughout the piece, but the top number shows a change in the number of beats in a measure.

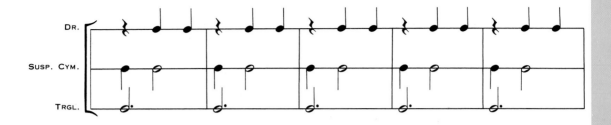

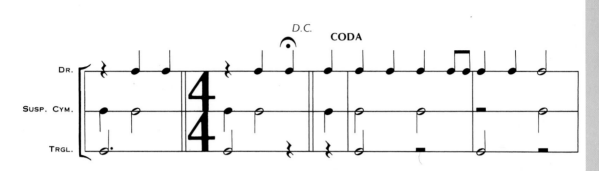

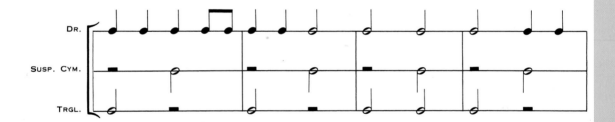

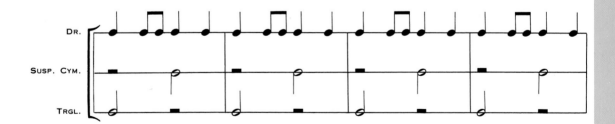

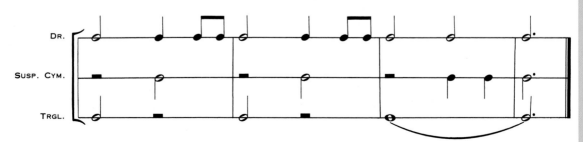

SIXTEENTH NOTES

While one person plays the steady beat on a drum, clap each of the lines below. Notice that the beat can be divided into
- two equal sounds ♪♪ eighth notes
- four equal sounds ♬♬ sixteenth notes

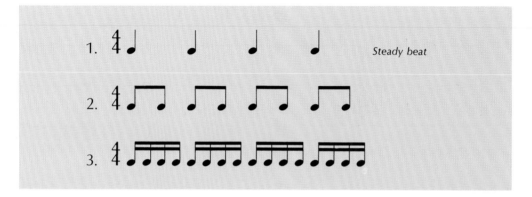

1. Steady beat

2.

3.

Now clap a pattern that uses both eighth notes and sixteenth notes to divide the beat.

4.

BATTLE HYMN OF THE REPUBLIC I <small>(SONG ON PAGE 113)</small>

Play this snare drum part to accompany the refrain of "Battle Hymn of the Republic."

SNARE DRUM

DOTTED RHYTHMS

A dot after a note makes it longer by half its value. Notice how dotted rhythms are used in songs you may know. Play these rhythms on any percussion instrument.

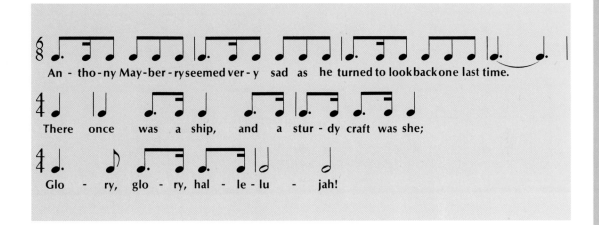

An - tho-ny May-ber-ry seemed ver-y sad as he turned to look back one last time.

There once was a ship, and a stur-dy craft was she;

Glo - ry, glo - ry, hal - le-lu - jah!

BATTLE HYMN OF THE REPUBLIC II (SONG ON PAGE 113)

Here are parts for small drum and cymbals. Add them to the snare drum part on page 230 and, with others, play an accompaniment for the refrain of "Battle Hymn of the Republic."

For the quarter rests (𝄽) in the cymbals part, dampen the sound by holding the cymbals against the body.

THE JOHN B. SAILS (SONG ON PAGE 14)

While listening to the recording of "The John B. Sails," play each line below on a muted cowbell. Notice that in line 4 the dot takes the place of the tie.

Play one of these parts as others sing "The John B. Sails." Someone can add the steady beat on the Autoharp. The chord letters in the music on page 14 show when to change from one chord to another.

232　Reading Rhythm

TILL THAT DAY BLUES <small>(Song on page 158)</small>

Practice one of these parts and play it with the recording of "Till That Day Blues," or form an ensemble with your friends to accompany the song in class.

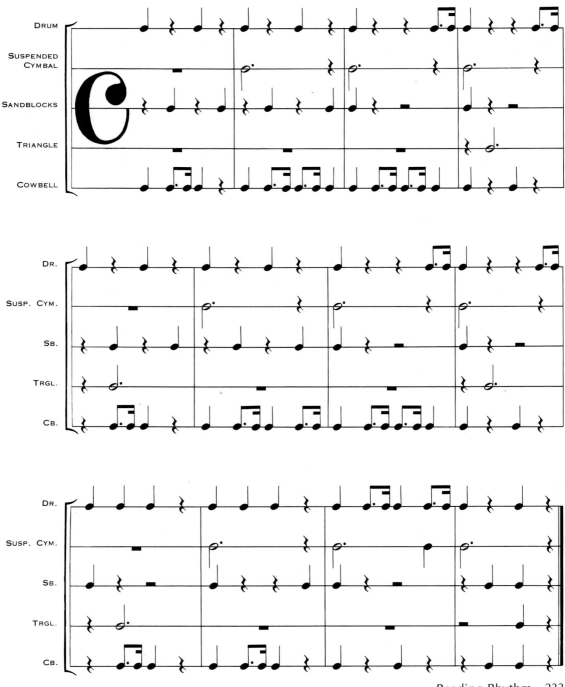

SYNCOPATION

Listen to the recording of "Artsa alinu" and play this pattern on a tambourine when it comes in the song.

(Art - sa   a - li - nu,   Art - sa   a - li - nu)

The special feeling of syncopation comes from playing some notes on the weak part of the beat. Clap the following lines to discover how a syncopated pattern develops from the steady beat.

ARTSA ALINU (SONG ON PAGE 81)

Practice one of the parts to play with the recording, or form an ensemble with your classmates to accompany the class singing of "Artsa alinu."

I'M GONNA SING OUT <small>(Song on page 142)</small>

Look through the claves part and notice that syncopation is created in two ways.

Sound on weak beats in section A

Silence on strong beats in section B

Practice syncopated patterns by playing the claves part. Then choose another part to add to the accompaniment.

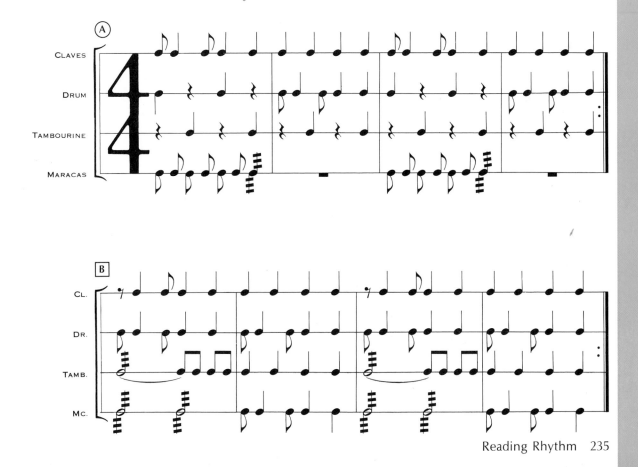

GREEN, GREEN (SONG ON PAGE 177)

Here is an arrangement you can use to accompany "Green, Green."
Be sure to follow the repeat signs.

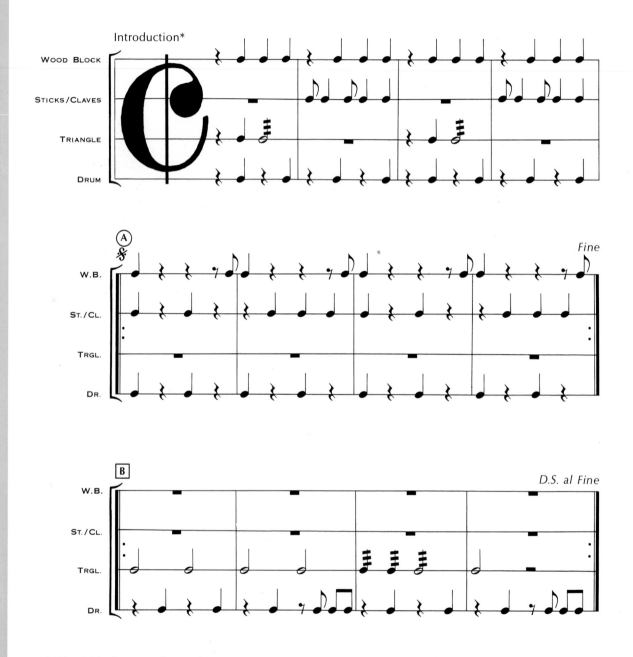

*Wood block enters first with voice 1; add sticks/claves with voice 2; add triangle and drum with voice 3.

WORKING WITH SOUNDS

⊙11   COMPILED BY DORIS HAYS

The world is full of sounds—sounds that can be organized in an endless variety of ways.

The following pages suggest ways in which you might choose and organize sounds. You might use tape recorders or voices or instruments, or a variety of ordinary objects around you.

Part of the excitement of learning about music is discovering the many ways in which composers use sounds.

Part of the excitement for *you* may be trying to use sounds in a way that no one else has thought of.

COMING TOGETHER, BY BOB BECKER

Here is a rhythm game for two players. Each player should:

1. Choose a number from 1 to 5. Don't tell the other player what your number is.

2. Clap a rhythm pattern that has as many beats as the number you chose, plus one beat of rest. For example, if your number is 4, your rhythm pattern would be

Both players together set a tempo and, beginning at the same time, clap their rhythm patterns over and over until they "come together." The patterns will come together when both players have a rest at the same time. If one player chooses number 4 and the other chooses number 3, the patterns would look like this:

Player 1:

Player 2:

As you clap your rhythm pattern, think of a new number between 1 and 5 so that when your rhythms come together you can begin to clap a new pattern without losing a beat.

Here is an example in another kind of notation. Each block stands for one beat. Empty blocks stand for rests.

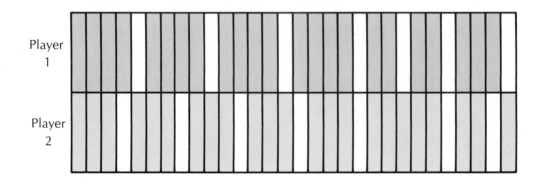

Player
1

Player
2

Find the places where the patterns come together.

Continue in this way until both of you choose the same number. When that happens, clap the rhythm pattern three times and stop. The game is over.

WAYS TO VARY "COMING TOGETHER"

1. Make the tempo twice as fast.

2. Accent some of the beats in your rhythm patterns, for example, the first and last beats.

3. Make your rhythm patterns more interesting. If you choose the number 3, clap ♩ ♫ ♩ 𝄽 instead of ♩ ♩ ♩ 𝄽

4. Play your rhythm patterns on a percussion instrument.

5. Play your rhythm patterns on a melody instrument; change to a new pitch each time you choose a new number.

6. Play the game with more than two players.
Can you think of other rhythm games to play? Can you think of ways to vary them?

IMPROVISE A RHYTHM ACCOMPANIMENT

Play a recording of your favorite song. As you listen, use a percussion instrument or a sound like clapping or pencil-tapping to discover different rhythm patterns that fit the song.

Try playing two different rhythm patterns one after the other to form a longer pattern. Notate your rhythm patterns so that another player can read and play them from your score.
You may use *traditional* notation or *graphic* notation. A rhythm pattern that looks like this in traditional notation

♫♩ , ♪ ♫♩ , ♪ ♫♩

might look like either of these in graphic notation.

LIGHT-SOUND-MOVEMENT

These symbols can be expressed in light, in sound, and in movement. As you move a flashlight beam across a dark surface, use the on-off button to turn the symbols into a "light design." How will you show the lines? the dots? How will you show "no light"? Experiment with moving the flashlight closer to the surface, then farther away.

Another time, turn the symbols into sound by playing an instrument. Which symbol will stand for a long sound? a short sound? Where will the pitch get higher? Where will it get lower? What will be the symbol for the loudest sound?

You can turn the symbols into movement by using a different body movement—bending, sliding, turning, etc.—for each symbol.

Have some friends help you turn the symbols into a light-sound-movement ensemble by doing all three activities at the same time.

Try making up new symbols that can be turned into a light design, into sound, and into movement. Have your friends help you interpret them in a light-sound-movement ensemble.

DANCE ON THE SPIRALS

BY DORIS HAYS   ©1979 DORIS HAYS

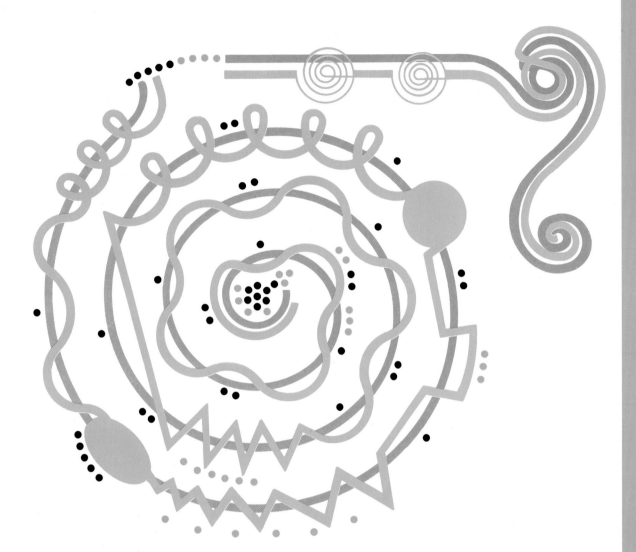

Dance on the Spirals combines light, sound, and movement. The red line stands for the motion of the dancer. The black dots stand for drum beats or triangle taps. The green dots stand for short flashes of light from a flashlight. The wash of blue color stands for the sweep of light from other flashlights around the dancer.

Do the dance starting from the center of the big spiral. Follow the lines around and out to the edge and top and over to the smaller spirals. Then try beginning at the outer edge and circling inward. Do the dance at different speeds.

FOLLOW THE LEADER, © 1973, BY DORIS HAYS

Use these symbols to write a piece for voices.

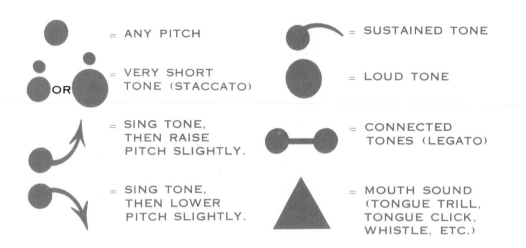

= ANY PITCH

= VERY SHORT TONE (STACCATO)

= SING TONE, THEN RAISE PITCH SLIGHTLY.

= SING TONE, THEN LOWER PITCH SLIGHTLY.

= SUSTAINED TONE

= LOUD TONE

= CONNECTED TONES (LEGATO)

= MOUTH SOUND (TONGUE TRILL, TONGUE CLICK, WHISTLE, ETC.)

Choose your "lyrics" from the following words and syllables.

SEE! OH? LAH! MMM! UGH!!! NOK! AH. . . MEE!

Your score might look something like this.

MMM!   MEE!   LAH!   MMM!   UGH!!!

When you have written your score, conduct a "follow-the-leader" performance of it. Choose five or more performers to stand in a semi-circle, facing you. Since the performers will be imitating your sounds, they will not need copies of your score. Perform the sounds in your score, one at a time. After each sound, signal the performers to imitate the sound you have made. Your signal should tell the performers whether you want them all to imitate your sound at the same time (ensemble) or whether you want each performer to imitate the sound alone, one after the other (in sequence).

MY NAME IS

FOR

1 OR MORE PERFORMERS
3 OR MORE TAPE RECORDERS
AND AUDIENCE

Members of the audience are recorded saying, "My name is —" (first name only).

Three or more identical tape loops are made from each "my name is—". This dubbing and editing process may be performed in view of the audience, and it may be done silently if the performer(s) wear earphones. Thus some other audible performance may happen simultaneously while this process is going on.

Each set of three or more identical loops is then played on three or more tape recorders for about two minutes or more. Because of slight differences in motor speed, tape tension and loop length (even in 'identical' loops) the loops proceed to move slowly in and out of phase with each other.

When changing from one set of loops to the next one should change one loop first, pause, then the second, pause, and then the third (and so on if there are more recorders). Eg., if set 1 has played for two minutes or more then the first loop of set 2 is substituted on the first recorder resulting in one loop of set 2 and two loops of set 1. Then the second recorder is changed resulting in two loops of set 2 and one of set 1. Finally the third recorder is changed resulting in three loops of set 2.

The piece is over when all sets of three or more loops have been played.

Steve Reich 5/67

ADAPTED FROM

MY NAME IS BY STEVE REICH
ACTIVITY 1

Here is one way to do *My Name Is*.

Make a tape recording of a friend saying his or her name, for instance, "My name is Rosalyn."

On separate tapes record two other friends saying their names. One might say, "My name is Fred." The other might say, "My name is Alice."

Make two copies of each recording. (When you copy the sounds from one tape onto another tape, you are *dubbing*.) You should have three tapes that say "My name is Rosalyn," three that say "My name is Fred," and three that say "My name is Alice."

Make each of the tapes into a tape loop. Directions for making tape loops are on page 119. Be certain that the three tape loops for each name are the same length.

Using three tape recorders, take the loops that say "My name is Rosalyn" and put one loop on each tape recorder. Start all three tape recorders at the same time. Let the loops play for two minutes.

Listen to the changes in sound as the loops play. At first, the names will all sound at the same time (*in phase*). As the loops continue to play, the names will not stay together—the loops will get *out of phase*.

This happens because one of the tape recorders may be running a little faster than the others, or because all the tape loops may not be exactly the same size.

At the end of two minutes, change to the tape loops that say "My name is Fred." Change the loop on one tape recorder at a time. As you change each loop, let the other two tape recorders keep playing. Let the "My name is Fred" loops play for two minutes.

After two minutes, change to the "My name is Alice" tape loops, one at a time. Let the loops play for two minutes.

To end the piece, turn the tape recorders off.

Listen to *My Name Is*. How is it like your piece? How is it different?

ACTIVITY 2

Here are some other things you can do with tape.

1. Make a version of *My Name Is* that uses more than three tape recorders and more than three tape loops for each name.

2. Join (splice) two or more *My Name Is* loops together to make a longer loop. For example, you might splice a "My name is Rosalyn" loop to a "My name is Fred" loop. Make a different loop for each tape recorder that you use. Plot a duration chart for each loop. If you use three tape recorders (TR's), your chart might look like this:

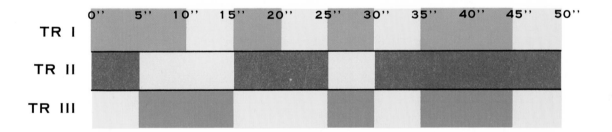

Control the length of sound from each tape recorder by fading the volume in and out.

3. Use tape loops of various lengths to experiment with other sounds besides voice. Some sound sources you might use are water dripping, water running, footsteps, whistling, paper crumpling, paper ripping, horn honking.

Try playing the sounds back at speeds that are faster or slower than the ones at which they were recorded.

ADAPTED FROM

ON THE WAY TO . . . , © 1973 BY DORIS HAYS

On the Way to . . . is a piece of music theater. It consists of a story that is "told" by a narrator and a piano. Read the story and then listen to it on the recording.

Every morning my brother and I get up early. We have eggs and cereal with bananas and milk for breakfast. After eating our eggs and our cereal with bananas and milk my brother and I get ready for school. My brother and I ride the bus to school when the weather is nice. On rainy days our father drives us to school so we don't get wet waiting for the bus. One rainy day when we were late for school my brother and I ran out the front door and slipped on a banana peel. Our father came running out the door behind us and he slipped on the banana peel. Our mother had just finished washing the dishes after our breakfast of eggs and cereal with bananas and milk when she noticed that we had forgotten our lunch. Our mother came running out the front door with our lunch and she slipped on the banana peel. I don't think I will ever forget that morning when my brother and I were late for school and we all slipped on a banana peel as we ran out the front door. My friend Marsha still can't understand why I yelled at her later that morning when she tried to share her lunch with me. All she said was, "Would you care for a banana?"

Try performing *On the Way to . . .* with some of your friends. Choose a different percussion instrument for each new underlined word in the story. For example, someone might play finger cymbals on the word "morning" or a wood block on the word "late." Try using hand sounds, too, and sounds that can be made with objects in the room. When you have assigned a sound to each word, choose someone to be narrator. As the narrator reads the story he should leave out the underlined words. An instrument should play whenever a word is left out. Try several different versions of *On the Way to . . .* to find the one you like best.

IMPROVISE ON A KEYBOARD INSTRUMENT

© 1973 Doris Hays

Experiment with playing single tones and clusters of tones in different places on a keyboard instrument (piano, organ, accordion, electronic keyboard, bells). Make up a sound pattern that uses clusters and single tones.

You may wish to notate your sound pattern so that you can remember it and so that others can play it. One way is to place symbols within a box.

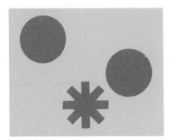

In this example, a dot (•) stands for a single tone, and a star (*) stands for a cluster of tones. The symbol near the top of the box stands for a high tone; the one near the bottom stands for low tones. The symbol halfway between the top and the bottom stands for a tone in the middle of the keyboard.

Follow the score for this sound pattern. Do you see the pattern of two high tones followed by a low cluster and a middle tone?

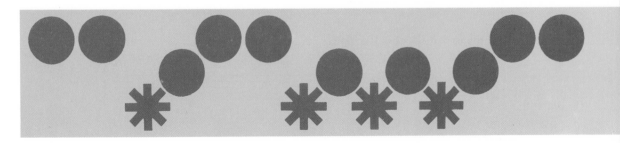

Now write your own sound pattern. You may use dots and stars, or any symbols that you like. Play your sound pattern on a keyboard instrument. Does it sound as good as it looks?

Working with Sounds 247

MAKE A MELODY—MAKE A SONG

© 1973 Doris Hays

Make up a melody of your own. If you like, you can choose the tones for your melody by chance. Tear a piece of paper into 14 smaller pieces. Write one tone name from A through G on each piece of paper. You should have two A's, two B's, two C's, and so forth.

Mix the papers and then close your eyes and pick 6 pieces, one at a time. The order in which you pick the tones will determine their order in your melody. If the first paper you pick says "C," C will be the first tone of your melody. If the second paper says "D," D will be the second tone of your melody.

After you've chosen your tones, experiment with different rhythm patterns. You may decide that your melody should have only quarter notes, as in this example.

Or you may want to give it a rhythm pattern that uses long and short sounds

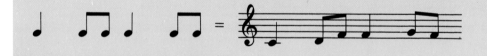

or a pattern that has a dotted rhythm.

Try putting words to your melody. You may have to change the rhythm of your melody a little to make the words fit.

Won-der what   this song   is?

Now try repeating the first two or three notes a few times before going on to the rest of the melody.

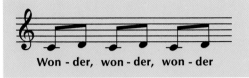

Won - der, won - der, won - der

Decorate your melody by adding some notes in between the original ones (ornamentation). Besides decorating the melody, the extra notes can make the words that are sung on them more important.

Won - der, won - der, won - der what _____ this song ____ is?

Play your melody to discover whether it falls into a pattern of strong beats and weak beats. Do the strong beats group the beats into sets of 2, 3, or 4? Write the meter signature next to the treble clef sign. Put a bar line before the note on the first beat in each set of 2, 3, or 4.

In this example, the beats fall into sets of 3. The meter signature is $\frac{3}{4}$

Won - der, won - der, won - der what _____ this song ____ is?

Now you have a good beginning for a song. Your melody can be the first phrase of the song. Repeat the phrase two or three times. Each time you repeat it, change it in some way. You can make the rhythm a little different or add some notes to the melody or take some notes away.

Make up a new phrase to end the first part of your song. Your ending phrase might be a contrasting phrase. If so, it will not sound like the phrases you've written so far.

Working with Sounds 249

One way to make a contrasting phrase is to write the notes of
the original phrase in reverse order (retrograde).

When you have your ending phrase, make up words for it. You
may have to repeat some tones or change the rhythm to make
your words fit.

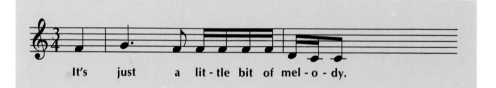

It's just a lit-tle bit of mel-o-dy.

Try adding some notes to "ornament" your closing phrase. You
may want to change the words slightly.

It's ___ just ___ a ___ lit-tle bit of mel-o-dy.

Now that you have the first part of your song, you can write the
rest of it by yourself. As you write, try some of the things that
you did in the first part of your song—use different rhythm
patterns; use ornamentation; repeat phrases, changing them in
some way.

Listen to *Wonder What This Song Is?* Is your song in the same
style, or is it in a different style?

◉ Hays: *Wonder What This Song Is?*

GLOSSARY

absolute music Music that has no suggestion of any nonmusical thing, idea, story, or event (*see* program music).

accent A single tone or chord louder than those around it.

accompaniment Music that supports the sound of a solo performer.

atonal Music in which no single tone is a "home base" or "resting place."

ballad In music, a song that tells a story.

beat A repeating pulse that can be felt in some music.

cadence A group of chords or notes at the end of a phrase or piece that gives a feeling of pausing or finishing.

call and response A musical device with a portion of a melody (call) followed by an answering portion (response). The response may imitate the call or it may be a separate melody that repeats each time.

canon A device in which a melody begins in one part, and then is imitated by other parts in an overlapping fashion (*see* round).

chant To sing in a manner approximating speech.

chord Three or more different tones played or sung together.

chord pattern An arrangement of chords into a small grouping, usually occurring often in a piece.

chorus (*See* refrain.)

clef A sign that tells where pitches are located on the staff. The sign 𝄞 (G clef, or treble clef) shows that G above middle C is on the second line. This clef is used for music in higher registers. The sign 𝄢 (F clef, or bass clef) shows the tone F below middle C on the fourth line. It is used for music in lower registers.

cluster A group of tones very close together performed at the same time; used mostly in modern music.

composer A person who makes up pieces of music by putting sounds together in his or her own way.

contour The "shape" of a melody, made by the way it moves upward and downward in steps and leaps, and by repeated tones.

contrast Two or more things that are different. In music, slow is a *contrast* to fast; section A is a *contrast* to section B.

countermelody A melody that is played or sung at the same time as the main melody.

density The thickness or thinness of sound.

duration The length of sounds, from very short to very long.

dynamics The loudness and softness of sounds.

elements The parts out of which whole works of art are made: for example, music uses the *elements* melody, rhythm, texture, tone color, form; painting uses line, color, space, shape, etc.

ensemble A group of players or singers.

fermata A sign (⌢) indicating that a note is held longer than its written note value, stopping or "holding" the beat.

frets Strips of metal across the fingerboard of guitars and similar instruments. The player raises the pitch of a string by pressing it into contact with a fret.

form The overall plan of a piece of music.

fugue A musical procedure based on imitation, in which the main melody (subject) and related melodies are repeated in higher and lower registers and in different keys. The texture is polyphonic.

ground A melody pattern repeated over and over in the bass (lowest part) of a piece, while other things happen above it.

harmony Two or more tones sounding at the same time.

improvisation Making up music as it is being performed; often used in jazz.

interval The distance between tones. The smallest interval in traditional Western music is the half-step (f–f♯, f♯–g, etc.), but contemporary music and music of other cultures often use smaller intervals.

jazz A style that grew out of the music of black Americans, then took many different substyles—ragtime, blues, cool jazz, swing, bebop, rock, etc.

key The particular scale on which a piece of music or section is based, named for its tonic, or key-tone, or "home-base" tone. (The key of D major indicates that the major scale starting and ending on the tone D is being used. *See* tonality.)

major scale An arrangement of eight tones in a scale according to the following intervals, or steps: whole, whole, half, whole, whole, whole, half.

251

measure A grouping of beats set off by bar lines.

melody A line of single tones that move upward, downward, or repeat.

melody pattern An arrangement of pitches into a small grouping, usually occurring often in a piece.

meter The way the beats of music are grouped, often in sets of two or in sets of three. The meter signature, or time signature, such as $\frac{3}{4}$ or $\frac{4}{4}$, tells how many beats are in the group, or measure (top number), and the kind of note that gets one beat (bottom number).

minor scale Several arrangements of eight tones in a scale, such as *natural minor* (whole, half, whole, whole, half, whole, whole) and *melodic minor* (upward: whole, half, whole, whole, whole, whole, half; downward: whole, whole, half, whole, whole, half, whole).

notes Symbols for sound in music.

octave The distance of eight steps from one tone to another that has the same letter name. On the staff these steps are shown by the lines and spaces. When notes are an *octave* apart, there are eight lines and spaces from one note to the other.

ornamentation In the arts, the addition of decorations, or embellishments, to the basic structure of the work.

ostinato A rhythmic or melodic phrase that keeps repeating throughout a piece or a section of a piece.

pattern In the arts, an arrangement of an element or elements into a grouping, usually occurring often in the work (see elements).

phrase A musical sentence. Each *phrase* expresses one thought. Music is made up of *phrases* that follow one another in a way that sounds right.

pitch The highness or lowness of a tone.

polyrhythm Several different rhythm patterns going on at the same time, often causing conflicts of meter among them.

program music Music that suggests or describes some nonmusical idea, story, or event (see absolute music).

range In a melody, the span from the lowest tone to the highest tone.

refrain A part of a song that repeats, with the same music and words. It is often called the "chorus," since it is usually sung by all the singers, while the verses in between are often sung by one voice.

register The pitch location of a group of tones (see pitch). If the group of tones are all high sounds, they are in a high *register*. If the group of tones are all low sounds, they are in a low *register*.

repetition Music that is the same, or almost the same, as music that was heard earlier.

rests Symbols for silences in music.

rhythm The way movement is organized in a piece of music, using beat, no beat, long and short sounds, meter, accents, no accents, tempo, syncopation, etc.

rhythm pattern A pattern of long and short sounds.

rondo A musical form in which a section is repeated, with contrasting sections in between (such as A B A C A).

round A kind of canon that leads back to the beginning of the melody and starts all over again (circle canon).

scale An arrangement of pitches from lower to higher according to a specific pattern of intervals. Major, minor, pentatonic, whole-tone, and chromatic are five kinds of scales. Each one has its own arrangement of pitches.

sequence The repetition of a melody pattern at a higher or lower pitch level.

solo Music for a single player or singer, often with an accompaniment.

staff A set of five horizontal lines on which music notes are written.

style The overall effect a work of art makes by the way its elements are used (see elements). When works of art use elements similarly, they are said to be "in the same style."

subject See fugue.

syncopation An arrangement of rhythm in which prominent or important tones begin on weak beats or weak parts of beats, giving a catchy, off-balance movement to the music.

tempo The speed of the beat in a piece of music (see beat).

texture The way melody and harmony go together: a melody alone, two or more melodies together, or a melody with chords.

theme An important melody that occurs several times in a piece of music.

tonal Music that focuses on one tone that is more important than the others—a "home base"—or resting tone.

tonality The kind of scale, major or minor, on which a piece of music or section is based (see key).

tone color The special sound that makes one instrument or voice sound different from another.

tone row An arrangement of the twelve tones of the chromatic scale into a series in which there is no focus on any one of them as the home tone. When the series is played backward, it is called the "retrograde."

triplet A rhythm pattern made by dividing a beat into three equal sounds.

variation Music that is repeated but changed in some important way.

INDEX

PICTURE CREDITS

3 4 5 6 7 8 9 10—RRD—88 87 86 85 84 83 82